The Streetcar Guide to New Orleans

The Streetcar Guide to New Orleans

By Earl W. Hampton, Jr., Louis Costa, Andre Neff, *and* Peter Raarup

PELICAN PUBLISHING COMPANY

GRETNA 2013

First edition, June 1980
Second printing, January 1981
Third printing, November 1981
Second edition, January 2013

The word "Pelican" and the depiction of a pelican are trademarks of Pelican Publishing Company, Inc., and are registered in the U.S. Patent and Trademark Office.

ISBN: 9781455614967
E-book ISBN: 9781455614974

Maps by Tina Luttrell except on pages 9 and 12

H. George Friedman provided some of the information on pages 13-14.

Printed in China

Published by Pelican Publishing Company, Inc.
1000 Burmaster Street, Gretna, Louisiana 70053

CONTENTS

INSTRUCTIONS

You can obtain your daily or weekly Jazzy Pass on any RTA vehicle, bus, or streetcar. Prices are $3 for the 1-day pass, $9 for the 3-day pass, and $55 for the 31-day pass. The passes can be used on any New Orleans Regional Transit Authority (NORTA) streetcar or bus. They save time, and you can avoid the hassle of having the exact fare ready every time you board.

If you do not wish to use a Jazzy Pass and do not have exact fare, you can insert a $5 bill for two people into the computerized fare box. It will issue you a credit for $2.50, which you can both use for your return trip.

This book provides maps to Uptown via the St. Charles streetcar, to the Mid-City area via the Canal Cemeteries and City Park lines, to the French Quarter via the Riverfront line, and to the train station via the Loyola Avenue line.

Visitors should begin with the Grand Tour of St. Charles Avenue. Board the streetcar either at stop 59 at Canal and Carondelet or stop 1 at St. Charles and Common. You are going uptown. Follow the instructions in blue.

NOTE: These streetcars are *not* tour vehicles. They are regular intercity commuter lines, and it is recommended to avoid rush hours if possible, as cars may be crowded. The best time to ride is between 9 a.m. and 3 p.m.

EMERGENCY INFORMATION

Police—504-821-2222 or 911
Emergency Medical Service—504-658-2640 or 911
Touro Emergency Room—504-897-7011

BOARDING THE STREETCAR

The streetcar stops only at car stops as shown in the key on page 17.

Board only at the front door. Insert your pass into the fare box; it will be returned to you right away.

ON BOARD THE STREETCAR

Move toward the rear, holding straps, poles, or brass handholds for safety. Be seated. Take notice which side you are sitting on, as you will wish to be on the opposite side for the return trip. Please save specially marked seats for handicapped or elderly.

On the older St. Charles cars, feel free to raise or lower windows and shades. The newer red Canal and Riverfront cars do not have shades, and on the Canal line, the cars are air-conditioned and heated, so the windows do not raise at all.

Smoking, radio playing, eating, and drinking are prohibited. Watch your children. Do not lean out of windows, as clearances are close with our beautiful oak trees.

GETTING OFF THE STREETCAR

Use this book's maps to decide where you would like to get off. Pull the signal cord to stop after passing the previous stop before your destination.

The signal cord is strung along the tops of the windows. In the rear, a signal button is located in the vestibule.

After signaling, move to the rear door. On the old, green, Perley Thomas streetcars on St. Charles, you must push the door when the green light above it goes on. On the newer Riverfront and Canal cars, the door is controlled by the operator. The streetcar cannot move while the door is open.

Once on the ground, do not cross the tracks until the streetcar has moved away.

LEGEND FOR ST. CHARLES STREETCAR INTERIOR

When green light over door lights up, push door open to exit from streetcar.

Button for signaling stop, to left of rear exit door.

Strap to hold if standing.

Pull cord briefly to signal for stop.

Adjust shade to see clearly.

Open or shut window as desired.

Brass handle for standees.

SCHEDULES and RIDING TIME

ST. CHARLES SCHEDULE

Average speed: 8.8-9.7 mph
7 days a week (total roundtrip is 13.13 miles)
6 a.m.- 8 p.m. every 10 minutes

LEONIDAS BUS SCHEDULE
(service to Audubon Zoo)

This bus line only runs weekdays, every 1 hour 10 minutes. The first bus going to the zoo from St. Charles and Broadway departs at 6:49 a.m., and the last one returning to the streetcar leaves the zoo at 6:42 p.m. All schedules are subject to change without notice.

This map shows the approximate time it takes to ride the St. Charles Streetcar to nine successive points along the route. The time markers are spaced at 5-minute intervals. The total time required to reach a given marker from Canal Street is also shown. This enables you to judge how long it will take to ride the streetcar between any 2 points along the route.

CANAL SCHEDULE

Length: About 4 miles (30 minutes each way)
6 a.m.-8 p.m.
Cemeteries: About every 10 minutes
City Park: About every 30-40 minutes

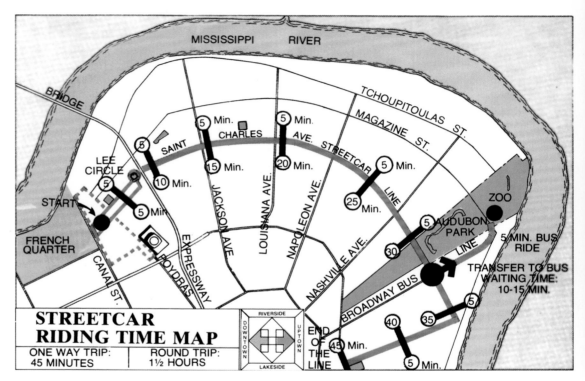

STREETCAR RIDING TIME MAP

ONE WAY TRIP: 45 MINUTES | ROUND TRIP: 1½ HOURS

RIVERFRONT SCHEDULE

Length: About 1.5 miles (20 minutes each way)
7 days a week
Basically no service after midnight
Every 20 minutes midday
Every 40 minutes early and late in the day

LOYOLA SCHEDULE

No schedule available at this writing

GETTING TO THE STREETCAR

Find your hotel or present location on the map. If in the French Quarter:

Walk to Royal or Bourbon and turn toward Canal Street. Walk uptown. If on Bourbon, simply cross Canal Street and wait there (stop 59, which is the end of the St. Charles line inbound and the beginning outbound). If on Royal, cross Canal and walk another block to Common (which is stop 1). St. Charles streetcars do not accept passengers at Canal and St. Charles. If you do not wish to purchase an all-day pass, the fare is $1.25 per person, exact change required. Or if you wish to board a Canal streetcar, simply make your way to Canal Street. The red cars stop at almost every corner.

Peak hours are Monday through Friday 6 a.m.-9 a.m. and 3 p.m.-6 p.m.

If in the Central Business District:

You can walk to any outbound stop along St. Charles Street (Union, Poydras, etc.) and board there. Of course, you can connect with St. Charles by using the red cars on Canal.

Not using a pass? Transfers are 25 cents extra, good in only one direction, and never on the same line.

HOTEL LIST

1. A Creole House
2. Andrew Jackson Hotel
3. Astor-Crowne Plaza
4. Best Western
5. Bienville House
6. Bourbon Orleans Hotel
7. Chateau Bourbon
8. Chateau Lemoyne
9. Chateau Motor Hotel
10. Comfort Inn
11. Cornstalk House
12. Dauphine Orleans Hotel
13. De La Post Motor Hotel
14. Doubletree
15. Embassy Suites
16. French Market Inn
17. Hilton Garden Inn
18. Hilton Riverside
19. Holiday Inn Loyola
20. Holiday Inn French Quarter
21. Hotel Le Cirque
22. Hotel Maison DeVille
23. Hyatt Regency
24. JW Marriott
25. Lafitte Guest House
26. Lafayette Hotel
27. Lamothe House
28. Le Pavillon Hotel
29. Le Richelieu Motor Hotel
30. Loew's
31. Maison Dupuy Hotel
32. Marriott
33. Monteleone Hotel
34. Place D'Armes Hotel
35. Prince Conti
36. Provincial Motor Hotel
37. Ramada Plaza Inn on Bourbon St
38. Ritz-Carlton
39. Roosevelt
40. Royal Orleans
41. Royal Sonesta Hotel
42. St. Ann Hotel/Marie Antoinette
43. St. Louis Hotel
44. St. Peter Guest Hotel
45. Sheraton
46. Ursuline Guest House
47. Warwick Hotel
48. Westin
49. W Hotel

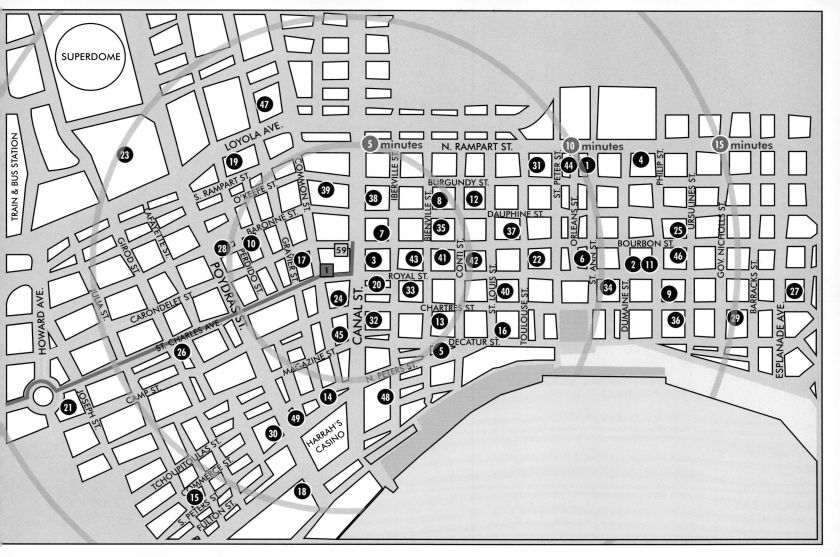

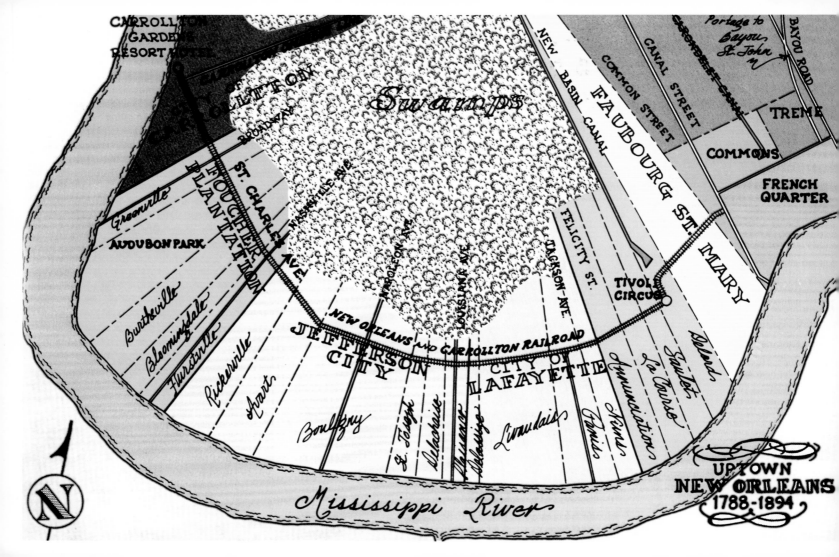

A ride on the green St. Charles Avenue Streetcar is a journey into the history and myth of New Orleans and a lesson in the development of a city. At the opposite end of the spectrum, a ride on our shiny new red cars on Canal Street evokes memories of old, while offering modern technology.

The green streetcars were built in 1923 and 1924 by the Perley Thomas Car Company. They are numbered in the 900 series and were designed by Perley A. Thomas of High Point, NC. The red streetcars are homemade, built right here in New Orleans by NORTA at the Carrollton car barn (Carrollton Station). While designed and built to look like our original streetcars, they are very modern, fast, and energy efficient. The ones on Canal Street, numbered in the 2000 series, have creature comforts such as air-conditioning and heating.

The St. Charles line has the distinction of being one of the oldest continuously operating rail lines in the world, established September 26, 1835. In the beginning, steam locomotives were used to pull passenger cars serving the towns of Lafayette, Jefferson City, and Carrollton. It was known then as the New Orleans & Carrollton Railroad (NO&CRR). That continuous record was interrupted by Hurricane Katrina.

GROWTH OF UPTOWN

To really understand how Uptown came to be, you have to go back to 1718 and the founding of New Orleans by Jean-Baptiste LeMoyne, Sieur de Bienville.

In the beginning, all Uptown was Bienville's plantation. The location of the original city, today's French Quarter, had been selected by Bienville in 1699. In 1718, John Law gave Bienville permission to build the city. The upriver boundary of the city plan is where Iberville Street is today, one block on the downtown side of Canal Street. From there to Common Street were the city walls and then the Commons. Through the Commons there was supposed to be a navigation canal connecting the river and Lake Pontchartrain. The canal was never constructed but gave Canal Street its name.

Beyond the city of Lafayette (today's Garden District) were scattered settlements and plantation homes and speculative subdivisions created by the owners of the NO&CRR. They were waiting for the land boom that the Carrollton line was expected to create, which eventually did come to pass.

The real growth of the street railway system began after the Civil War. The 1860s ushered in great experiments with technology. The first major technical change was the replacement of the old steam engines with horses in 1867. In 1885, two electric trains were shown at the World's Industrial and Cotton Centennial Exposition in Audubon Park. One of those was an electric trolley designed by a company in Belgium. Montgomery, AL adopted this system the next year, but it would be almost a decade before trolleys ran in the city of New Orleans.

On February 1, 1893, the Carrollton line was renamed St. Charles, and new streetcars began service. They left from Carrollton Car House, which is still in use today. In 1899, NO&CRR and Canal & Claiborne Railway consolidated to become a company known as NO & Carrollton RR, Light & Power. It went into receivership in 1905 and emerged as New Orleans Railway & Light. A complete and final reorganization of all street railways and power companies was done in 1922.

Street railway mileage in the city reached a peak that year with 225 miles of track. In 1926, the highest ridership occurred, with 148 million patrons. That was surpassed in 1945 with 246 million riders. After the war, trolley lines that had held on to help the war effort disappeared along with ridership. New Orleans Public Service, Inc. ran our transit system until 1983, when it turned over operations to the government-subsidized NORTA. By then, New Orleans had only one trolley line left, the St. Charles line.

CANAL STREET HISTORY

Canal Street—at 170 feet 6 inches the widest business-district street in the country—was never paved curb to curb for the use of ordinary vehicles. It began as a "commons" area between the original city, also called the French Quarter or Vieux Carré, and the American Quarter, which developed immediately upriver. In the early 1800s, a canal was supposed to have been built down the middle of this commons. It never came to pass, and the commons evolved into a street, with two roadways flanking a central reservation.

This "neutral ground" (as New Orleanians call the median) originally sported grass and trees, providing an almost parklike environment. And like on some of New Orleans' other wide streets, part of this neutral ground was eventually laid with street railway tracks, free from conflict with other types of vehicles. But because Canal was (and remains) the heart of the Central Business District, its wide neutral ground became completely filled with tracks and was finally paved over. Even paved, though, the neutral ground was still for street railways only, and other vehicles remained in the two flanking roadways.

Street railways were a part of the Canal Street scene until May 31, 1964, when the Canal line was dieselized. The inner tracks and the four-track terminus and loop at the Liberty Monument were removed, and in their place, bus lanes were installed from Claiborne to the Liberty Monument. This marked the first time that any vehicle other than a streetcar had the right to operate on the neutral ground of Canal Street. The only track remaining on Canal Street was the single block of outer track between Carondelet and St. Charles, which did not even have a passenger boarding area.

RIVERFRONT STREETCAR LINE

August 14, 1988, saw the inauguration of the first new streetcar line in New Orleans since 1926.

The Riverfront line used a section of standard-gauge track that was no longer needed by the railroads. It was operated with 3 Perley Thomas cars and 3 secondhand cars from Melbourne, Australia, the latter being wheelchair accessible. The Riverfront line proved to be an immediate success both with tourists and New Orleanians, so it was expanded to 2 separate tracks in 1990. The Perley Thomas cars were retired in 1997 when the line was changed to a wider gauge. New cars (replicas of the 900-series Perley Thomas cars used on the St. Charles line) were built in Carrollton Station. Today there are 7 cars assigned to the Riverfront line, numbered 457 to 463, all of them completely wheelchair accessible. Cars 458 to 463 are newly built. The other car, the 457, is an original 1924 Perley Thomas car (formerly the 957) rebuilt for operation on the Riverfront line.

CANAL STREETCAR COMEBACK

In 1997, it was decided to build new tracks connecting the Riverfront line with the St. Charles line, so that Riverfront cars could be housed at Carrollton Station. Double track was built on Canal Street, using the bus lanes in the inner-track position, from Baronne/Dauphine to the foot of Canal, and connected to the Riverfront line, which was converted to wider gauge. The main Canal line would extend from the foot of Canal Street out to City Park Avenue, just as it had before dieselization in 1964. There would also be a branch line along North Carrollton Avenue, which had never had streetcar service, to Esplanade Avenue at Beauregard Circle.

Local oilman and philanthropist Patrick F. Taylor donated $1.2 million worth of surplus oilfield pipe to be used as support poles for the trolley wires. A prototype Perley Thomas replica car, number 2001, had been constructed in 1997, featuring wheelchair accessibility, air-conditioning, and what was described as state-of-the-art control technology from the Czech Republic, including dynamic braking. Under the direction of Elmer Von Dullen, 23 additional streetcars, numbered 2002 to 2024, were constructed at Carrollton Station to equip the Canal line. The Brookville Mining Equipment Corp. provided 23 sets of four-motor trucks, controls, and air-conditioning units for the new cars. The line reopened in 2004.

LOYOLA AVENUE STREETCAR LINE

At this writing, the newest streetcar line in New Orleans is under construction. It will run on Loyola Avenue between Canal Street and the Union Passenger Terminal. Construction is slated to be completed by December of 2012. It will service the New Orleans Public Library, City Hall, the Superdome, the Hyatt Hotel, and the Amtrak train/Greyhound bus station. Costing slightly more than $34 million, it will use surplus red Canal cars. The line will be 8 blocks long with 4 stops (Tulane Avenue, Poydras Street, Julia Street, and the Union Passenger Terminal).

The Streetcar Guide to New Orleans

GRAND TOUR OF ST. CHARLES AVENUE

The maps in this book show the entire routes of the St. Charles, Canal Street, Riverfront, and Loyola streetcar lines. The St. Charles line begins at car stop 59 at Carondelet and Canal or car stop 1 at St. Charles and Common, going all the way to the end of the line (Carrollton and Claiborne) and back. Part of the Leonidas bus line takes you from St. Charles and Broadway to the Audubon Zoo.

The key shows the symbols used on the Atlas Maps. Maps of New Orleans are usually oriented to the north with the river at the bottom. The St. Charles Atlas Maps in this book have the river at the top to allow the direction of travel to proceed from left to right on the page as you look from car stop 59 or 1 in the Central Business District to Uptown.

MAPS

Map 1—Central Business District
Map 2—Coliseum Square
Map 3—Garden District
Map 4—Bouligny
Map 5—University Section
Map 6—Leonidas Bus, Audubon Park, Zoo
Map 7—Riverbend
Map 8—Carrollton

KEY

— Uptown/Lakebound Streetcar route.

— Downtown/Riverbound Streetcar route.

■ Uptown/Lakebound car stop.

▪ Downtown/Riverbound car stop.

• • • Walking route.

1 Hundred block.

This compass rose is provided on each map in the book.

In New Orleans major directions are Up, Down, River, and Lake.

Up means upriver from any point.

Down means downriver from any point.

Uptown is the area upriver from Canal Street.

River is to the left as you travel Up.

Lake is to the right as you travel Up.

This tour provides a sample of the attractions of Uptown New Orleans. The route takes you the entire length of our historic St. Charles Streetcar line past gracious homes, fine restaurants, and shopping. The upbound route beginning at car stop 59 or 1 is in blue on the maps. If you are starting your tour uptown, turn to page 56 and follow the yellow route.

LEGEND TO MAP 1

CAR STOP 59
corner Canal and Carondelet streets

1 PICKWICK CLUB
corner Canal Street and St. Charles Avenue

CAR STOP 3
Poydras Street

2 ONE SHELL SQUARE
corner Poydras Street and St. Charles Avenue

3 PAN AMERICAN LIFE INSURANCE BUILDING
opposite One Shell Square

CAR STOP 4
Lafayette Street

4 GALLIER HALL
545 St. Charles Avenue

5 LAFAYETTE SQUARE

6 FEDERAL COURT OF APPEALS/OLD POST OFFICE
600 Camp Street

7 U.S. DISTRICT COURT/HALE BOGGS BUILDING
500 Camp Street

8 ST. PATRICK'S CATHOLIC CHURCH
724 Camp Street

CAR STOP 5
Julia Street

9 JULIA ROW
600 block Julia Street

10 LOUISIANA CHILDREN'S MUSEUM
420 Julia Street

CAR STOP 6
St. Joseph Street

11 CONTEMPORARY ARTS CENTER
900 Camp Street

CAR STOP 7
Lee Circle

12 LEE CIRCLE

13 OGDEN MUSEUM OF SOUTHERN ART
925 Camp Street

14 CIVIL WAR MUSEUM
929 Camp Street

15 WORLD WAR II MUSEUM
945 Magazine Street

Contemporary Arts Center

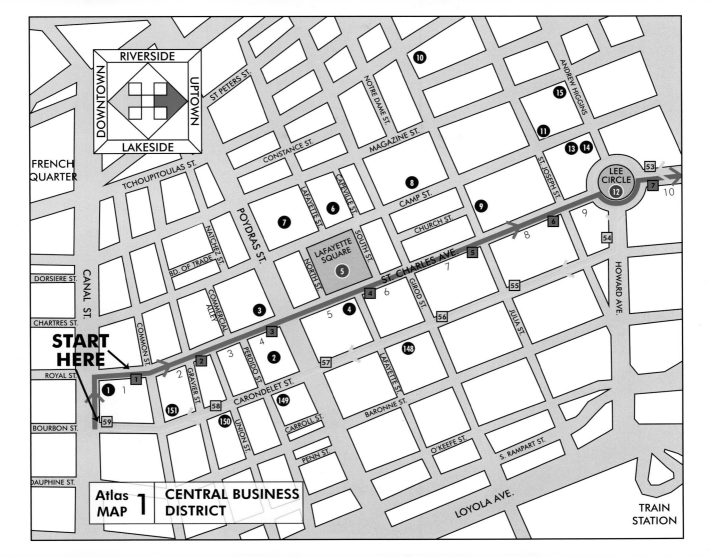

RIVERSIDE
DOWNTOWN
UPTOWN
LAKESIDE

FRENCH QUARTER

ST PETERS ST.

TCHOUPITOULAS ST.

CONSTANCE ST.

NOTRE DAME ST.

MAGAZINE ST.

ANDREW HIGGINS

CAMP ST.

CHURCH ST.

LAFAYETTE ST.

CAPEVILLE ST.

POYDRAS ST.

NATCHEZ ST.

BD. OF TRADE

COMMERCIAL ALLEY

NORTH ST.

SOUTH ST.

LAFAYETTE SQUARE

ST. CHARLES AVE.

ST. JOSEPH ST.

LEE CIRCLE

HOWARD AVE.

DORSIERE ST.

CANAL ST.

CHARTRES ST.

START HERE

COMMON ST.

GRAVIER ST.

PERDIDO ST.

CARONDELET ST.

CARROLL ST.

BARONNE ST.

GIROD ST.

JULIA ST.

ROYAL ST.

BOURBON ST.

UNION ST.

PENN ST.

O'KEEFE ST.

S. RAMPART ST.

DAUPHINE ST.

Atlas
MAP 1   CENTRAL BUSINESS DISTRICT

LOYOLA AVE.

TRAIN STATION

Begin Upbound tour.

Board the streetcar at car stop 59 or car stop 1 (see "Getting to the Streetcar" for instructions on reaching these locations from your hotel).

CAR STOP 59 CANAL AND CARONDELET
1 PICKWICK CLUB
corner Canal and St. Charles

Built in 1826 and converted to a hotel in 1858, the present elaborate façade in the Italianate style dates from 1875, when it became the Crescent Billiard Hall. The architect was Henry Howard, known for his designs of many later plantation homes as well as numerous commercial and residential buildings in the city. The upper floors have served as a clubhouse of the Pickwick Club, a private organization, since 1950. During Mardi Gras season, a grandstand on Canal Street is the scene of ceremonies and festivities.

CAR STOP 3 POYDRAS STREET
2 ONE SHELL SQUARE
corner Poydras and St. Charles

Completed in 1972, this skyscraper of 50 stories (697 feet) is the tallest building in New Orleans. It rests on 500 concrete friction piles, each 210 feet long, topped by 8 feet of concrete. This extensive foundation system makes possible buildings of any height in a city with a high water level and soil so soft that 4-story buildings were once considered folly.

3 PAN AMERICAN LIFE INSURANCE BUILDING
opposite One Shell Square

This 27-story building, faced in red granite, was completed in 1980. Its outstanding features include an energy-efficient heating and cooling system and 2 large interior atriums.

CAR STOP 4 LAFAYETTE STREET

Get off here and cross St. Charles Avenue into the square. Reboard at the same location or stops 5, 6, or 7. This shows the benefits of a 1-day pass.

4 GALLIER HALL
545 St. Charles

Begun in 1845 and completed in 1853, this building served as City Hall for 100 years.

Gallier Hall, 1853

Today it is a city office building and public hall named in honor of its architect, James Gallier, Sr. During Mardi Gras, the mayor greets kings and queens of the various parades from a grandstand erected in front.

Gallier Hall is considered one of the finest examples of Greek Revival architecture in the country. The figures in the tympanum over the colonnade are Justice, flanked by America, representing Liberty, and Louisiana, representing Commerce.

5 LAFAYETTE SQUARE
Bounded by St. Charles, Camp, North, and South

This is the original Plaza of the Ville Gravier, laid out in 1788. After 1852, the second municipality chose Lafayette Square as the site of their new City Hall, which became the seat of the government for the united city. The statues in the square are of Benjamin Franklin, Henry Clay, and John McDonough, a benefactor of local public schools. Clay's statue once stood at the corner of Canal Street and St. Charles Avenue. Today Lafayette Square is surrounded by several government buildings.

6 FEDERAL COURT OF APPEALS/OLD POST OFFICE
600 Camp

Designed by Hale and Rogers and built in 1914, it is the city's outstanding example of Beaux Arts architecture, drawing strongly on the traditions of the Italian Renaissance. Each corner of the roof has sculpture representing History, Industry, Commerce, and the Arts. It was built as the main U.S. Post Office and was converted to a Federal Courthouse in 1961.

7 U.S. DISTRICT COURT/HALE BOGGS BUILDING
500 Camp

This complex was completed in 1976. The office tower is a memorial to Hale Boggs, the U.S. congressman from the Second District of Louisiana who died in a plane crash in Alaska.

8 ST. PATRICK'S CATHOLIC CHURCH
724 Camp

Look to the left after crossing Girod Street. Over the rooflines of the 19th-century buildings on Camp Street, you will see the Gothic Revival tower of St. Patrick's Church. Begun in 1838 and completed in 1840, this was the first Roman Catholic church in New Orleans to be built outside the French Quarter. Its congregation was primarily Irish.

CAR STOP 5 JULIA STREET
9 JULIA ROW
600 block Julia

Built in 1833, this fine row of simple, yet elegant townhouses is the only remaining example

Julia Row, 1833

Civil War and Ogden museums

of a popular housing type from the boom years of the 1830s. Originally, each of the 13 houses was a single-family residence and was occupied by a wealthy or notable family.

10 LOUISIANA CHILDREN'S MUSEUM
420 Julia

Walk 2 blocks toward the river and you will encounter the Louisiana Children's Museum. It is fun for all ages, and your child can even pretend to be a streetcar motorman.

CAR STOP 6 ST. JOSEPH STREET
11 CONTEMPORARY ARTS CENTER
900 Camp

One block toward the river is the Contemporary Arts Center.

Lee Circle, gateway to Uptown
CAR STOP 7 LEE CIRCLE
12 LEE CIRCLE
intersection of Howard and St. Charles

This monument to Robert E. Lee, commander of the Confederate Army, was completed in 1884 by sculptor Alexander Doyle. The general faces north, which, in addition to expressing defiance to his enemies, provides the only easily located orientation in the city to a cardinal direction.

Lee Circle is the gateway to Uptown and is part of the neoclassical street pattern of the surrounding area. Originally it was known as Tivoli Circus and was to have been an amusement park surrounded by a moat that was part of the drainage system. If you look to your right as you round Lee Circle in a counterclockwise direction, you can catch a glimpse of the golden-domed St. John the Baptist Catholic Church (sounds oxymoronic, doesn't it?), closed after Hurricane Katrina; the Plaza Tower, a 45-story office building also closed; and Union Passenger Terminal for Amtrak trains and Greyhound buses, end of the future Loyola streetcar line.

13 OGDEN MUSEUM OF SOUTHERN ART
925 Camp

14 CIVIL WAR MUSEUM
929 Camp

15 WORLD WAR II MUSEUM
945 Magazine

This complex consists of 4 museums within a 2-block radius, all very worthwhile, with something for everyone.

LEGEND TO MAP 2

CAR STOP 8
Erato Street

16 JERUSALEM TEMPLE
1137 St. Charles Avenue

CAR STOP 9
Melpomene Street

16B HEIRLOOM FURNISHINGS
www.heirloomfurnishings.com

16C TOWN AND COUNTRY BRIDAL
www.townandcountrybridal.com

16D HOSHUN RESTAURANT
www.hoshunrestaurant.com

16E PLEASE U RESTAURANT
1751 St. Charles Avenue

17 SIMMONS HOUSE
1347 Coliseum Street

18 LOERBER HOUSE
1629 Coliseum Street

19 GRAHAM'S ROW
1430-32 Euterpe Street

20 FREEDMAN'S BUREAU
1420 Euterpe Street

21 ALLEN HOUSE
1703 Coliseum Street

22 STRACHAN HOUSE
1717 Coliseum Street

23 COLISEUM SQUARE

24 WILSON HOUSE
1741 Coliseum Street

25 GRACE KING HOUSE
1749 Coliseum Street

26 MOORE-CAFFERY-BAKER HOUSE
1228 Race Street

27 McCONNELL HOUSE
1472 Camp Street

28 BLANCHARD HOUSE
1125 Race Street

29 ST. VINCENT'S GUEST HOUSE
1507 Magazine Street

30 ARCHIBALD-BOULWARE HOUSE
1531 Camp Street

31 GHOST HOUSE
1221 Orange Street

CAR STOP 11
Felicity Street

32 FRERET HOUSE
1309 Felicity Street

33 FELICITY METHODIST CHURCH
corner Felicity and Chestnut Streets

34 McGINTY HOUSE
1332 Felicity Street

35 BLAFER HOUSE
1328 Felicity Street

36 FLOWER-MORRISON HOUSE
1805 Coliseum Street

37 NORWEGIAN SEAMEN'S CHURCH
1772 Prytania Street

38 ST. ANNA'S RESIDENCE
1823 Prytania Street

CAR STOP 12
St. Andrew Street

39 SEDGEBEER HOUSE
1533 St. Andrew Street

40 ZION LUTHERAN CHURCH
1924 St. Charles Avenue

CAR STOP 13
Josephine Street

41 EIFFEL SOCIETY
2040 St. Charles Avenue

42 PONTCHARTRAIN HOTEL
2031 St. Charles Avenue

Moore-Caffery-Baker House, 1867

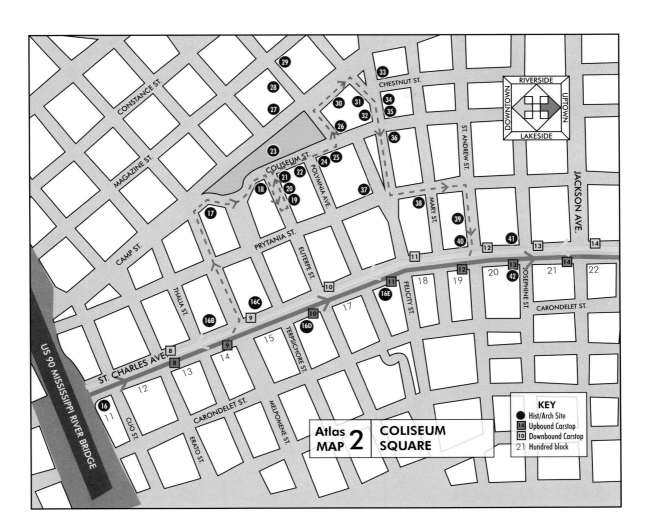

CONSTANCE ST.

CHESTNUT ST.

RIVERSIDE

DOWNTOWN · UPTOWN

LAKESIDE

MAGAZINE ST.

COLISEUM ST.

POLYMNIA AVE.

ST. ANDREW ST.

JACKSON AVE.

CAMP ST.

PRYTANIA ST.

EUTERPE ST.

MARY ST.

THALIA ST.

ST. CHARLES AVE.

TERPSICHORE ST.

FELICITY ST.

CARONDELET ST.

JOSEPHINE ST.

CARONDELET ST.

CLIO ST.

CARONDELET ST.

MELPOMENE ST.

ERATO ST.

US 90 MISSISSIPPI RIVER BRIDGE

Atlas **2** MAP

COLISEUM SQUARE

KEY

● Hist/Arch Site

14 Upbound Carstop

10 Downbound Carstop

21 Hundred block

CAR STOP 8 ERATO STREET
16 JERUSALEM TEMPLE
1137 St. Charles

Built from plans by Emile Weil and Sam Stone dated 1916 as the headquarters of the Ancient Arabic Order Nobles of the Mystic Shrine, it is a fanciful structure that combines the eclecticism of the period with the iconography of the Shriners. Notice the desert scene over the main entrance.

CAR STOP 9 COLISEUM SQUARE WALKING TOUR

Melpomene and Terpsichore are the Muses of Tragedy and Dance. They are two of the nine Muses of Greek mythology for whom the streets crossing St. Charles in this area are named. Prytania Street is named for the Prytaneum, a college for classic scholars that was never built.

Most of the neighborhood known today as Coliseum Square, or the Lower Garden District, was laid out in 1806 for four Creole plantation owners who wished to develop their land for the expanding city.

In those days, only three years after the Louisiana Purchase, when the city was entering its greatest period of growth, classic ideas and architecture were the rage, especially in the United States, of which New Orleans was now a part, and France, which was the social model of the Creoles. St. Charles Avenue was known as Nayades Street. Nayades are water nymphs. Dryades, wood nymphs, also had a street that still bears their name but was closer to the woods on the lake side of St. Charles Avenue.

To take the Coliseum Square walking tour, get off at **CAR STOP 9 MELPOMENE STREET,** walk toward the river 2 blocks to Coliseum Street, and turn right.

17 SIMMONS HOUSE
1347 Coliseum

An unusual house in that, on the one hand, it is a typical detached Greek Revival villa, but on the other, it displays differences dictated by the odd shape of its lot overlooking Coliseum Square. Notice the excellent etched-glass door, a late-19th-century addition.

18 LOERBER HOUSE
1629 Coliseum

It was built circa 1880 in what was known as the Newport style, a combination of the eclectic Queen Anne style with Georgian Revival details in celebration of the United States Centennial. Originally it was the home of Fredrick Loerber, a prominent surgeon.

Turn right and walk a half-block.
19 GRAHAM'S ROW
1430-32 Euterpe

Built in 1857, there were originally 3 houses in a row, but 1 was destroyed by fire in 1971. The buildings are Greek Revival but display the elaborate detail of the Italianate style. The builder, Dr. Graham, was killed in a duel over an allegedly rigged election for coroner in which he ran and lost. Soon after, the Civil War brought financial ruin to

Mrs. Graham, who, as a paragon of the mid-19th-century Southern lady, finally restored the family fortunes.

20 FREEDMAN'S BUREAU
1420 Euterpe

A Greek Revival house dating from 1847, its history is filled with the tumult of Civil War occupation. The home of the Thornhill family, who were prominent in the cotton trade, it was seized by General Butler and used as an office of the Bureau of Refugees, Freedmen, and Abandoned Lands, the first social-service agency of the U.S. government. After Reconstruction it was returned to the family, who lived there for a total of almost 90 years. Today it has been restored essentially to its original appearance. The exterior colors and the oak graining on the doors date to the early years of the Thornhills' residence.

Return to Coliseum Street.
21 ALLEN HOUSE
1703 Coliseum

An interesting example of 19th-century architecture and renovation, this house is believed to have been a simple Greek Revival built around 1850. It was later renovated in the Italianate style. Still later, the stained-glass window was added.

Strachan House, circa 1850

22 STRACHAN HOUSE
1717 Coliseum

Built circa 1850, this house is of the typical plan of the period. It has a hall along the side of double parlors and a dining room at the end of the hall in the service wing. However, it displays eccentric detailing that is not Greek Revival and resembles the use of brackets popular in the later Italianate style.

23 COLISEUM SQUARE
Bounded by Coliseum, Race, and Camp

Coliseum Square is the center of the neighborhood known by the same name. The neighborhood is listed on the National Register of Historic Places, not only because of the wonderful architecture but also because of the park and street plan. Originally there was to be an elaborate system of basins, fountains, canals, parks, and public buildings. Most of these did not develop as planned because the area did not become urban until the 1840s, but the drainage system and the streets that change direction to accommodate the bend in the river remain. The "square" occupies the original Coliseum Place, the curved area you enter that was to contain a huge fountain, and the site of the Coliseum. Like the Prytaneum, it was never built.

Greek Revival was the most popular architectural style in New Orleans from about 1840 into the 1860s, the period of many of the homes in Coliseum Square. However as time passed, other styles, especially Italianate and then Queen Anne, began to be popular. As a result, many of the houses are a composite of several different styles. The most popular combination is Greek columns and the very Italianate detail of curved tops on windows.

Wilson House, 1847

24 WILSON HOUSE
1741 Coliseum

Built in 1847, the correct Doric and Ionic capitals on the columns and the simple but generous proportions mark this house as an outstanding example of Greek Revival style. Notice the large live oak in the front garden, planted in 1880 and a member of the Live Oak Society.

Grace King House, 1849

25 GRACE KING HOUSE
1749 Coliseum

From 1904 to 1932 it was the home of Miss King, author of numerous romances of the Old South. This house was a gathering place for the literary establishment of that period. It was built in 1849 and was originally a rather simple Greek Revival building, similar to the Wilson House. Elaborate remodeling was carried out in 1871 by a Northern merchant who made a fortune in the shoe business during Reconstruction.

26 MOORE-CAFFERY-BAKER HOUSE
1228 Race

Completed in 1867, this outstanding residence is a composite of the Greek Revival and Italianate styles. It was designed by Henry Howard, the architect of many plantation homes. One legend tells of its foundation being used as a public meeting place during the occupation of New Orleans.

Walk riverbound on Race to see the next 3 landmarks.

27 McCONNELL HOUSE
1427 Camp

A good example of the use of Italianate details on an essentially Greek Revival building, this house was built in 1869 for a Mrs. Terence McConnell.

28 BLANCHARD HOUSE
1125 Race

This handsome Greek Revival home has been added to over the years. The original brick house, now only the dining room, was built in 1843. In 1853, the wood-frame main house was added in the front. Although it is a single-family dwelling, a 1920s addition remains from when it served 2 families. The large live oaks are said to date from 1872. Notice the diamond-patterned wood rail, an early detail frequently replaced by cast iron.

29 ST. VINCENT'S GUEST HOUSE
1507 Magazine

Constructed in 1864, this is an impressive example of mid-19th-century institutional design in the Italianate style with cast-iron balconies. It was designed by Thomas Milligan, who was the architect for many Roman Catholic institutions at that time.

Walk back to Camp, cross Camp, and turn left.

30 ARCHIBALD-BOULWARE HOUSE
1531 Camp

Built in the 1850s, this fine Greek Revival home is distinguished by its exposed brick façade, a construction technique little used in Louisiana because it required imported bricks. Local bricks were usually too soft to be exposed to the elements, which accounts for the stucco finish on most of the older masonry buildings. By the time of this construction, local bricks could be left exposed but did not give the precise lines desired. Notice the difference in texture between the front walls of imported brick and side walls of local material. In the 1880s it became the home of William H. Bofinger, president of the American District Telephone Company.

Turn right onto Orange.

31 GHOST HOUSE
1221 Orange

Although the house is quite beautiful architecturally, the overgrown tropical garden filled with palms gives the property a haunted air. One of the oldest houses in Coliseum Square, it probably dates back to the 1840s but is documented as of 1853, the year the Greek Revival porch was added. Its historical interest comes from having been the home of the Coleman family, who frequently entertained George Washington Cable and other literary figures. It was confiscated during the occupation of New Orleans and served as a residence for General Butler's staff officers.

A verified manifestation of the supernatural is its most interesting attribute. On certain evenings of the week one is prevented from entering a certain bedroom by what is said to be the spirit of a lady's maid protecting her mistress, allegedly a young woman who went mad when her newborn baby was taken from her.

CAR STOP 11 FELICITY STREET
32 FRERET HOUSE
1309 Felicity

Built in 1880 by James Freret for his family, but probably never occupied by them, it is unique in New Orleans as an example of an Italianate villa. Most Italianate architecture in New Orleans was a style of detail applied to the traditional house form that evolved early in the 19th century, but this house is Italianate in form as well.

Turn left on Felicity and walk a half-block.

33 FELICITY METHODIST CHURCH
corner Felicity and Chestnut

Built in 1888, it replaces an older church destroyed by fire the year before. Unfortunately the Gothic spires were lost in a hurricane.

Walk back lakebound toward St. Charles on Felicity.

34 McGINTY HOUSE
1332 Felicity

It was built 1870 in the typically New Orleans form of Italianate. Notice the unusually slender columns on the upper balcony and the exceptionally elaborate details around the door.

35 BLAFER HOUSE
1328 Felicity

Built in 1869, again in the Italianate style, this house is notable as an authentic restoration, including its unusual colors.

36 FLOWER-MORRISON HOUSE
1805 Coliseum

Built circa 1860, this house is essentially Greek Revival and, unlike the others seen so far, is a raised cottage. This building type is one in which all the principal rooms are on a single floor that is raised a considerable height above the ground. Building in this manner was a necessity in the earliest days of the city because of the danger of flooding, but later it came to be simply a style. In New Orleans terminology, a cottage is any house with one principal floor, whether raised or not. This house has been the home of two mayors of the city, Walter C. Flower and deLesseps S. Morrison.

Walk to Prytania and look to your right.
37 NORWEGIAN SEAMEN'S CHURCH
1772 Prytania

Built in contemporary Scandinavian style, the church is an interesting institution that provides a home away from home for Norwegian seamen.

Turn left on Prytania and go up 1 block.
38 ST. ANNA'S RESIDENCE
1823 Prytania

An outstanding Greek Revival building built in 1850 by the Society for the Relief of Destitute Females and Their Helpless Children, it is now a home for the elderly.

Continue 1 more block uptown to St. Andrew and turn right lakebound toward St. Charles.
CAR STOP 12 ST. ANDREW STREET
39 SEDGEBEER HOUSE
1533 St. Andrew

Built in the Italianate style of the 1870s, the house has been given a later appearance by the generously proportioned front porch added in the 1890s. The outstanding features are the original frescoed ceilings and the early 20th century murals by John Sedgebeer, a former resident of the house and a decorator of numerous churches and public places.

Zion Lutheran Church
40 ZION LUTHERAN CHURCH
1924 St. Charles

Designed by architect Albert Deittel and dedicated in 1871, this Gothic Revival structure is a reminder of the character of St. Charles Avenue of the past. The congregation was founded in 1847, and their first church was at Euterpe and Baronne streets.

GREATER NEW ORLEANS TOURIST AND CONVENTION COMMISSION
2020 St. Charles

It is open weekdays, 8:30 a.m.-5 p.m. Stop in if you need some help along the way.

Board an Uptown-bound St. Charles Avenue Streetcar.
CAR STOP 13 JOSEPHINE STREET
41 EIFFEL SOCIETY
2040 St. Charles

One part of this building, which was constructed to look similar to the Eiffel Tower, is original to that Parisian tower—the actual restaurant was moved to New Orleans in the mid-1980s. During a 1981 structural renovation of the Eiffel Tower, all 1,100 steel panels and 30,000 bolts of its 562-foot-level restaurant were disassembled. The plan was to put it on street level near the tower, but governmental agencies blocked the owner from using the original name, which quashed the project. So, like a giant erector set, the original restaurant from the Paris landmark was reconstructed on St. Charles Avenue. The building is now a special-events venue.

42 PONTCHARTRAIN HOTEL
2031 St. Charles

LEGEND TO MAP 3

CAR STOP 15
First Street

43 DIOCESAN HOUSE
2265 St. Charles Avenue

44 HACKETT COTTAGE
2336 St. Charles Avenue

45 2344 ST. CHARLES AVENUE

46 LOUISE S. McGEHEE SCHOOL
2343 Prytania Street

47 TOBY'S CORNER
2340 Prytania Street

48 ADAMS HOUSE
2423 Prytania Street

49 MADDOX HOUSE
2507 Prytania Street

50 WOMEN'S OPERA GUILD
2504 Prytania Street

CAR STOP 16
Third Street

51 EWIN HOUSE
2520 Prytania Street

52 OUR MOTHER OF PERPETUAL HELP CHAPEL
2521 Prytania Street

53 BRIGGS-STAUB HOUSE
2605 Prytania Street

54 VILLERE-CARR HOUSE
2621 Prytania Street

55 COLONEL SHORT'S VILLA
1448 Fourth Street

CAR STOP 17
Washington Avenue

56 THE RINK
2727 Prytania Street

56B GARDEN DISTRICT BOOK SHOP
www.GardenDistrictBookShop.com

56C JUDY AT THE RINK
2727 Prytania Street

57 BEHRMAN GYM
1500 Washington Avenue

58 LAFAYETTE CEMETERY
1400 Washington Avenue

59 FRERET'S FOLLY
2700-26 Coliseum Street

60 EUSTIS-KOCH HOUSE
2627 Coliseum Street

61 WILLIAMS-WHITE HOUSE
2618 Coliseum Street

62 ROBINSON HOUSE
1415 Third Street

63 MUSSON HOUSE
1331 Third Street

64 MORRIS-ISRAEL HOUSE
1331 First Street

65 WHITE HOUSE
1312 First Street

66 CARROLL HOUSE
1315 First Street

67 ROSEGATE
1239 First Street

68 PAYNE-STRACHAN HOUSE
1134 First Street

69 MONTGOMERY HOUSE
1213 Third Street

70 GENERAL HOOD HOUSE
1206 Third Street

71 DAMERON HOUSE
2524 St. Charles Avenue

72 MORRIS HOUSE
2525 St. Charles Avenue

73 GRIMA HOUSE
2701 St. Charles Avenue

74 LAFAYETTE DAIRY/GROSE HOUSE
1616 Washington Avenue

CAR STOP 18
Sixth Street

75 CHRIST CHURCH CATHEDRAL
2919 St. Charles Avenue

CAR STOP 19
Harmony Street

76 VAN BENTHUYSEN-ELMS MANSION
3029 St. Charles Avenue

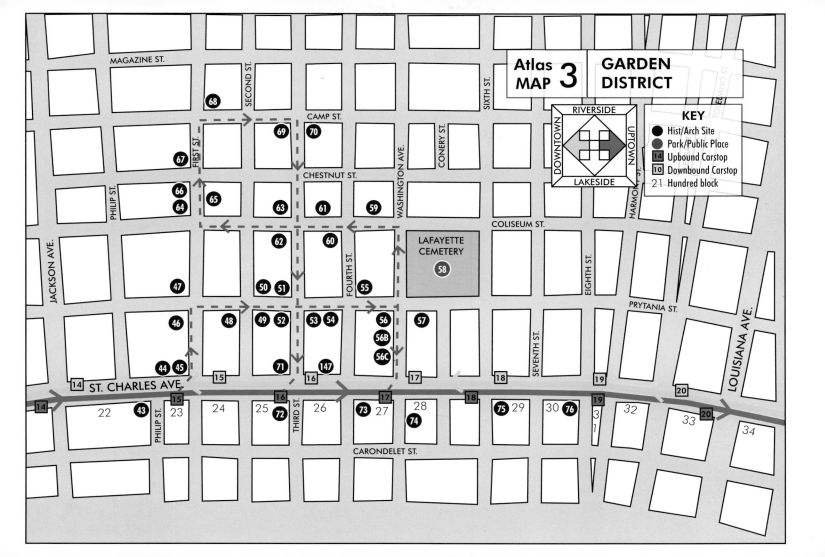

CAR STOP 15 GARDEN DISTRICT WALKING TOUR

As you cross Jackson Avenue, you enter the Garden District. The site numbers are in order of the suggested walking tour.

Get off at **CAR STOP 15 FIRST STREET.** Before venturing into the Garden District, look at the 3 sights listed below.

43 DIOCESAN HOUSE

2265 St. Charles

Built in the year 1856-57 for Miss Lavinia C. Dabney by the firm of Gallier & Turpin, it is a magnificent example of Greek Revival architecture. Occupied for many years by the family of Jonas V. Rosenthal, it was purchased in 1952 by the Episcopal Diocese of Louisiana and used by them for 2 decades. Today it is again a private home.

44 HACKETT COTTAGE

2336 St. Charles

Built in 1854 for another maiden lady, Miss Susan Hackett, it is a fine example of a Greek Revival cottage from the early days of the Garden District.

45 2344 ST. CHARLES AVENUE

This large home of the mid-19th century, despite its fine proportions and commanding location, is not well known historically. It probably dates from the 1850s, a decade in which style was still Greek but fancy detail was used lavishly. Numerous later additions to the rear are interesting also.

Walk riverbound on First Street into the heart of the Garden District. The Garden District was once the fashionable part of the city of Lafayette annexed to the City of New Orleans in 1852 and is still one of the most desirable residential areas in New Orleans. The heart of the area was once the plantation of Celeste de Marigny Enoul de Livaudais, who left her husband to live in the court of King Louis Philippe of France.

Unlike Coliseum Square, which contains modest homes and commercial buildings side by side with mansions, the Garden District originally had very large lots, only 4 to a block, which led to its being the first neighborhood with all houses, or villas as these detached homes were then known, set in gardens. The Garden District is listed on the National Register of Historic Places.

46 LOUISE S. McGEHEE SCHOOL

2343 Prytania

Built in 1872 for Bradish Johnson, popularly known as the Indigo King, it was designed by James Freret in the Renaissance Revival style, which was basically an elaboration of the Italianate. It was used as a private home until 1929, when it became McGehee's School, an exclusive girls' school.

47 TOBY'S CORNER

2340 Prytania

Built in 1838, it is probably the oldest house in the Garden District. It is a Greek Revival cottage with simple details on a rather large scale. The ample grounds are surrounded by the original picket fence and contain the Livaudais Oak, another member of the Live Oak Society. This site is one of the few remaining examples of the one-quarter-block building lots in the original Garden District, which ensured that only the wealthy would build in the neighborhood.

The house acquired its name from the original owners, Mr. and Mrs. Thomas Toby, and the fact that its corner location was long the only landmark in the area primarily developed 20 year later. Thomas Toby came to New Orleans from Philadelphia in 1817 and became quite prosperous but lost his fortune financing the Texas Revolution.

Walk Uptown bound on Prytania. The next cross street is Second.

48 ADAMS HOUSE

2423 Prytania

Built in 1860, this large home of the cottage type is in the Greek Revival style and is notable for its large garden and the circular bay window on the Uptown side.

49 MADDOX HOUSE

2507 Prytania

Built in 1852 for Joseph H. Maddox, editor of the *New Orleans Daily Crescent*, a leading newspaper of the time, it is in the Greek Revival style. Its rooms have unusual proportions, based on 11-foot squares. The parlors are 22x44; the library and dining room are 22x22. More common dimensions for the parlors would be 20x50 and the other two rooms would be 20x25.

Adams House, 1860

Women's Guild of the New Orleans Opera Association, 1858

50 WOMEN'S GUILD OF THE NEW ORLEANS OPERA ASSOCIATION
2504 Prytania

Originally it was built for the Davis family in 1858 in the Greek Revival style. Late in the 19th century, the house was enlarged by the addition of a music room, dining room, and more bedrooms housed in and behind the octagonal turret on the Uptown side. Also, a conservatory was added in the rear. The last private owners, the Seebold family, decorated the interior lavishly, and, upon Mrs. Seebold's death, bequeathed it to the Guild.

It is open for tours Monday only 10 a.m.-noon and 1-4 p.m. Nominal admission.

CAR STOP 16 THIRD STREET
51 EWIN HOUSE
2520 Prytania

Built in 1853, this house has a less formal plan than most as is evident from its asymmetrical façade. Notice the fine pair of beveled and leaded-glass front doors, not original to the house but one of its notable features.

52 OUR MOTHER OF PERPETUAL HELP CHAPEL
2521 Prytania

Formerly a chapel for the Garden District, this was originally a private residence, built in 1856. It is an early example of a design that became popular later, a masonry house with balconies of cast iron rather than wood.

During the Colonial Period and first half of the 19th century, wood was the more commonly used material for balcony railings and other exterior elements. At that time iron railings were wrought iron, which was expensive and used primarily on public and commercial buildings. However, in the mid-19th century, cast iron entered the market and was an instant success in New Orleans, which led to "iron lacework" becoming a symbol of the city.

The reason for this great popularity was not only its decorative nature, but also the columns that cast-iron technology supplied. Wide balconies often cover the sidewalks in the French Quarter and the Central Business District, adding living space and protecting the pedestrian. These were made possible by cast-iron columns, not subject to rot like wood. This house, though a villa set in a garden, is an example of this exuberant use of cast iron at that time.

The archdiocese has moved the chapel from Prytania to St. Mary's Chapel, 1516 Jackson Avenue. This little church was moved from Lafayette Cemetery No. 2 on Washington Avenue to its present location on Jackson, which probably saved it from the floodwaters of Hurricane Katrina.

After its longtime use as a chapel, the Prytania building was owned by author Anne Rice and later actor Nicolas Cage.

53 BRIGGS-STAUB HOUSE
2605 Prytania

Described in 1854 as "the most tasteful in the entire suburb," this Gothic Revival house is one of the few residences in New Orleans in this style. It was built circa 1849.

54 VILLERE-CARR HOUSE
2621 Prytania

Built circa 1870, this eclectic, late-19th-century version of the older Greek Revival mansions is interesting architecturally.

55 COL. SHORT'S VILLA
1448 Fourth

Also known as the Cornstalk Fence House, it was designed by Henry Howard in 1859. Its outstanding feature is the cast-iron fence in the cornstalk pattern, which is quite realistic and includes entwined morning glories and pumpkins at the base of the posts. Like most unusual things in New Orleans, it has a legend.

Col. Short's Villa, 1859

The story claims the fence was specially designed by the colonel to keep his wife from being homesick for Iowa.

Walk uptown on Prytania Street 1 block to Washington.

CAR STOP 17 WASHINGTON AVENUE
56 THE RINK
2727 Prytania

Built circa 1885 as the Crescent City Skating Rink, it now houses specialty shops. The Rink was constructed at the same time as the World's Industrial and Cotton Centennial Exposition farther uptown. The owner sought to attract Exposition visitors passing on the Prytania Streetcar. However, neither she nor the Exposition promoters were successful. In 1891, the building became S. Johnson & Sons, a prominent firm of morticians and embalming. With its proximity to Lafayette Cemetery, it became a very successful endeavor. In 1920, it became an automobile garage and remained so until its restoration in 1979.

57 BEHRMAN GYM
1500 Washington

This building was the Southern Athletic Club, where Gentleman Jim Corbett trained for his 1892 World Championship fight with John L. Sullivan in New Orleans. The gymnasium itself has been torn down and the front renovated into a private residence.

Walk riverbound on Washington Avenue for half a block.

58 LAFAYETTE CEMETERY
1400 block of Washington

Laid out in 1833, it was the burial ground for the city of Lafayette. New Orleans cemeteries are unusual by American standards in that most burials, and essentially all in the 19th century, are above the ground. The basic unit is the family tomb, typically a freestanding structure of brick or stone that contains space for 2 or more caskets. These tombs are used for generations as decomposition is rapid in the hot, humid climate. Older remains are dropped to a crypt below each tomb to make space for the new burials.

Other structures in the cemeteries are the wall units or ovens that frequently form the outer walls. In Lafayette Cemetery, these form the Washington Avenue wall and are used by poorer families. Finally, there are society tombs, similar in design to the ovens but freestanding. These belong to religious, civic, benevolent, military, and other groups. One society tomb in Lafayette Cemetery is also one of its finest monuments. It is the Jefferson Fire Company #22 tomb showing an 1830s pumper in marble relief.

The rather unusual method of burial developed from several factors. Most commonly cited is the high water table, which makes burial in the ground difficult without lining the grave with masonry. Other strong influences, however, were the traditions of France and Germany, from which most of the early settlers came, and the fact that it conserves land, a precious commodity in a city built on the narrow alluvial banks of a river and surrounded by water, marsh, and swamp.

You have 2 options at this point in the walking tour. If your time is limited, simply walk lakebound 1.5 blocks, back to St. Charles Avenue. At the Washington Avenue streetcar stop, you can choose to go farther uptown or return downtown. If you wish to continue the Garden District walking tour, walk riverbound on Washington to the corner of Coliseum Street and turn left.

59 FRERET'S FOLLY
2700-26 Coliseum

These 5 almost identical Greek Revival houses were built in the 1860s as a spectacular venture by architect William A. Freret, the older brother of the builder of Freret House, at 1309 Felicity Street (see map 2). His own home was the Freret Mansion, at 1525 Louisiana Avenue.

Eustis-Koch House

60 EUSTIS-KOCH HOUSE
2627 Coliseum

A unique home with Swiss chalet-style decorative details on the gables, the house itself is a more typical mid-19th-century building in the picturesque style of the 1860s and 1870s. Richard Eustis, a U.S. ambassador to France, lived here for many years. More recently it belonged to Richard Koch, one of the leading restoration architects of his generation. Movie actress Sandra Bullock now owns the home.

61 WILLIAMS-WHITE HOUSE
2618 Coliseum Street

This simple, finely proportioned Greek Revival house features a magnificent live oak in the front yard. It was once a hotel and faced Third Street. The front yard was sold in the 1870s to build the house now on the corner, which accounts for the unusual "side" entrance to the house.

Robinson House, 1865

62 ROBINSON HOUSE
1415 Third

One of the most beautiful houses in the city, it is attributed to the architect Henry Howard. It was built in 1865 for Walter G. Robinson, a Virginia tobacco merchant. When viewing houses of this size, it is always interesting to remember that they have very few rooms. The original plan here was only 8 rooms for the family, 2 on each side of the hall on each floor. The kitchen, pantry, stable, and servants' quarters occupied the service wing to the side.

63 MUSSON HOUSE
1331 Third

This is an early example of the Italianate style, built circa 1853. The original bay windows on the façade were removed in 1884, when the cast-iron balcony was erected. It was built for Michel Musson, postmaster of New Orleans and uncle of French painter Edgar Degas. Although Degas lived on Esplanade Avenue with his brother during his visits to New Orleans, he was a frequent guest in his uncle's home. The Mussons were a Creole family who were an exception to the rule that Uptown was only for Americans in the 19th century.

Continue downtown bound on Coliseum for 2 blocks to First Street. Turn right on First Street, toward the river.

Morris-Israel House, circa 1869

64 MORRIS-ISRAEL HOUSE
1331 First

Built circa 1869 by the same builder as Carroll House down the block, and at approximately the same time, this beautiful house is only half as large and lost its garden to a neighboring lot, a common situation as the fortunes of the original owners rose and fell.

White House, circa 1849

65 WHITE HOUSE
1312 First

This house is interesting primarily for its architectural history. Built circa 1849 as a 1.5-story raised cottage facing Chestnut, it was turned to its present location, raised a full story, and given a new façade in 1878.

66 CARROLL HOUSE
1315 First

Constructed in 1869 in the Italianate style with a cast-iron balcony, this house is notable for having maintained its original large garden and many of the original plantings. Notice the especially well proportioned carriage house on Chestnut Street.

67 ROSEGATE
1239 First Street

This very fine Greek Revival house of the 1850s originally had a garden stretching an entire block to Camp Street. Notice the fence, said to be the precursor of today's chain-link fences. It is identical to the fences of the newer homes on the block and once defined the property. Author Anne Rice owned this property at one time.

68 PAYNE-STRACHAN HOUSE
1134 First

Perhaps the finest example of Greek Revival residential architecture in New Orleans and noted for its exquisite garden hidden behind the fence, it was built in 1849. The major historical event associated with the house is the death of Jefferson Davis, president of the Confederacy. He became ill and died while he was visiting the owner, Judge Fenner, in 1889.

Walk Uptown bound on Camp Street 2 blocks to Third Street.

69 MONTGOMERY HOUSE
1213 Third

This fine house in the picturesque style was built for Archibald Montgomery circa 1868. The architect is unknown, but the design is similar to the work of Calvert Vaux, a popular architect in the East at this time.

70 GENERAL HOOD HOUSE
1206 Third

Built in 1852, this unusual house, although partially altered, still displays a sense of grandeur. The double bays and their mansard roofs are precursors of the Second Empire style of 20 years later and may be later additions. Gen. John Bell Hood moved to New Orleans after the Civil War, as did many Southern leaders, because the economy, though depressed by New Orleans standards, was healthy for the South. He entered the cotton business, married, and fathered 11 children. Tragically, Gen. and Mrs. Hood and their daughter died of yellow fever in 1879.

Turn lakebound on Third Street and walk 4 blocks to St. Charles Avenue.

71 DAMERON HOUSE
2524 St. Charles

The exact construction date and the name of the original occupant are lost. One legend is that Bernard de Marigny, a very colorful character of 19th-century New Orleans and a brother of Celeste Livaudais, once lived here. James Dameron bought, or possibly built, the house in 1861. Used as a school from 1923 to 1953, it is again a private home. It is probably the most beautiful Greek Revival house remaining on the Avenue.

72 MORRIS HOUSE
2525 St. Charles

Some believe that the original house, probably dating from 1885 and the largest remaining home designed by Thomas Sully, is included on the site. Legend says that the first owner's wife was too superstitious to allow demolition. The lower floor does contain Greek Revival design elements, which lends validity to the theory of 2 houses in 1. You may see Mardi Gras flags flying here. A former monarch of the Krewe of Rex must have lived here, with the krewe even altering its parade route in order to include a toast at this home.

Board an Uptown-bound streetcar here at car stop 16 to continue the tour. At this point in the tour, numerically listed attractions will be on the lakeside only, so choose your seat so that when seated facing forward, you will be on the right side of the car. If you can wait for a near-empty car, do so.

73 GRIMA HOUSE
2701 St. Charles

The garden of this house is one of the most beautiful in New Orleans. Built in 1850, the home is a fine example of Greek Revival architecture. It was renovated late in the 19th century to combine both Italianate and Second Empire details. Unlike most renovations, this one is an unqualified success. Be sure to note the fine plasterwork on the corners.

74 LAFAYETTE DAIRY/GROSE HOUSE
1616 Washington

Built in the mid-19th century, this impressive house served as dairy offices for an unknown company in the city of Lafayette. It faced St. Charles Avenue but was turned in the 1910s to make room for the apartment complex now on the corner. Notice the gargoyles near the roof. The building was also the home of Lillian S. Grose, who has been a tremendous help in getting this book and a previous one together.

Christ Church Cathedral, 1887

CAR STOP 18 SIXTH STREET
75 CHRIST CHURCH CATHEDRAL
2919 St. Charles

The 4th church to serve as the Cathedral for the Episcopal Diocese of Louisiana, this impressive Gothic Revival building was completed in 1887. Its tower was once crowned by a roof that, like many New Orleans church steeples, was lost in a hurricane.

Van Benthuysen-Elms Mansion, 1869

CAR STOP 19 HARMONY STREET
76 VAN BENTHUYSEN-ELMS MANSION
3029 St. Charles

It was built in 1869 in the Italianate style for Watson Van Benthuysen, a relative of Jefferson Davis who lived here until he died in 1901. Mr. Van Benthuysen was at one point president of the NO&CRR, which evolved into the streetcar line you are now riding. From 1931 until the start of World War II, the home served as the German consulate. It was a private residence from 1952 to 1968, when, at the death of John Elms, the family started to use the property for private functions such as wedding receptions.

LEGEND TO MAP 4

CAR STOP 21
  Foucher Street

**77 CHURCH OF JESUS CHRIST OF THE
  LATTER DAY SAINTS**
  3613 St. Charles Avenue

CAR STOP 22
  Peniston Street

78 CUTHBERT BULLITT HOUSE
  3637 Carondelet Street

79 THE COLUMNS
  3811 St. Charles Avenue

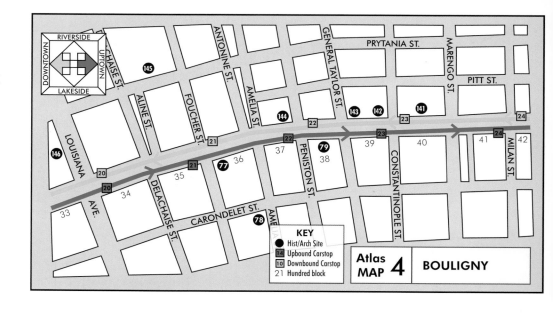

KEY
Hist/Arch Site
Upbound Carstop
Downbound Carstop
21 Hundred block

Atlas MAP 4 BOULIGNY

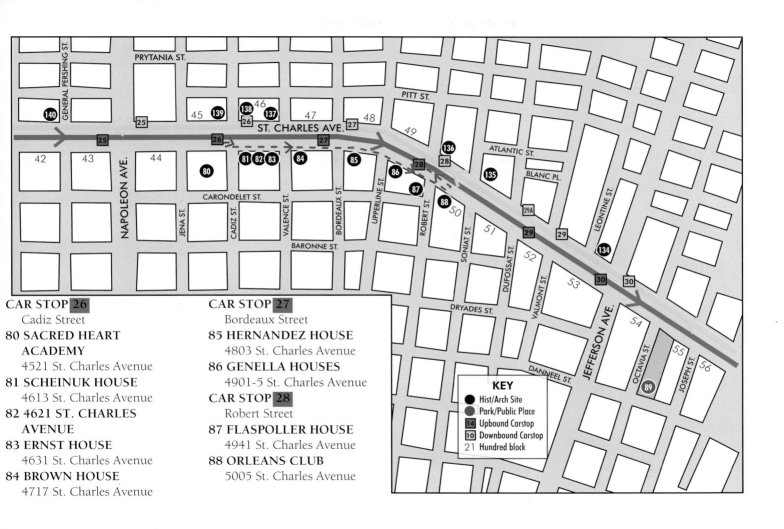

CAR STOP 26
Cadiz Street

80 SACRED HEART ACADEMY
4521 St. Charles Avenue

81 SCHEINUK HOUSE
4613 St. Charles Avenue

82 4621 ST. CHARLES AVENUE

83 ERNST HOUSE
4631 St. Charles Avenue

84 BROWN HOUSE
4717 St. Charles Avenue

CAR STOP 27
Bordeaux Street

85 HERNANDEZ HOUSE
4803 St. Charles Avenue

86 GENELLA HOUSES
4901-5 St. Charles Avenue

CAR STOP 28
Robert Street

87 FLASPOLLER HOUSE
4941 St. Charles Avenue

88 ORLEANS CLUB
5005 St. Charles Avenue

KEY
- ● Hist/Arch Site
- ● Park/Public Place
- 14 Upbound Carstop
- 10 Downbound Carstop
- 21 Hundred block

The Columns, 1884

CAR STOP 21 FOUCHER STREET
77 CHURCH OF JESUS CHRIST AND THE LATTER DAY SAINTS
3613 St. Charles

78 CUTHBERT BULLITT HOUSE
3637 Carondelet

Once situated on St. Charles Avenue on the site of the Columns, it was moved about 1880. It was built circa 1868 in the Swiss Chalet style and is sometimes referred to as the Cuckoo Clock House.

CAR STOP 22 PENISTON STREET
79 THE COLUMNS
3811 St. Charles

This huge home on the original site of the Cuthbert Bullitt House was built in 1884. Legend tells us it was a wedding present. In the 1970s an impressive battle was waged to save it from demolition. Architecturally it began as an Italianate-style building with a tower designed by Thomas Sully. The huge, 2-story columns and porch were added and the tower was removed later, probably in the 20th century when it was popular to copy Colonial and Greek Revival styles. The interior was used in the filming of the movie *Pretty Baby*.

To take the Bouligny walking tour, get off at **CAR STOP 26 CADIZ STREET.** The area known as Faubourg Bouligny was laid out in 1834 as a land development tied to the NO&CRR (predecessor of the St. Charles streetcar).

Sacred Heart Academy, 1899

80 SACRED HEART ACADEMY

4521 St. Charles

Built in 1899 on the site of an orange plantation purchased by Les Mesdames de Sacre Coeur in 1887, the location was the suggestion of the archbishop who wished to avoid a conflict between various teaching orders who wished to settle in the Garden District.

The Convent, designed by Owen & Diboll, is considered to be one of the finest buildings on St. Charles Avenue, with its large garden and symmetrical wings surrounded by a colonnade. It is one of the more exclusive girls' schools in New Orleans.

81 SCHEINUK HOUSE

4613 St. Charles

Built circa 1870, this small but finely detailed house in the Italianate style is one of the older homes on this part of the Avenue.

82 4621 ST. CHARLES AVENUE

Little is known of this house, but its style is sufficiently antique that it could have been built in the 1850s. The gingerbread brackets are probably later additions.

83 ERNST HOUSE

4631 St. Charles

Built circa 1900 in the Georgian Revival style, it generated considerable attention on December 7, 1941. Its resident at the time, the consul general of Japan, had his staff throw the files into the driveway and set them on fire. Today it is a private residence again.

Brown House, 1902

84 BROWN HOUSE

4717 St. Charles

Easily the largest mansion remaining on the Avenue, it was built in 1902 by William P. Brown as a wedding present to his bride. It cost $250,000 and took 5 years to build, a considerable expenditure of both money and time for that period. It is in the Romanesque Revival style in close imitation of the work of Henry Hobson Richardson.

CAR STOP 27 BORDEAUX STREET
85 HERNANDEZ HOUSE

4803 St. Charles

Built circa 1860 and renovated to its present appearance a decade later, it was the home of Joseph Hernandez, the president of the NO&CRR in the latter years of the 19th century. It is one of the few mansard-roofed, Second Empire-style houses remaining in New Orleans. For many years it was part of a boys' school, but the barracks-style building on the Avenue was torn down in the 1960s, and the house was restored and moved closer to St. Charles.

86 GENELLA HOUSES

4901-5 St. Charles

These 2 almost identical houses were built circa 1885 on the same lot as a speculative venture and caused a great legal conflict when sold to different owners. Notice the fine magnolia trees in front of the houses on this block.

CAR STOP 28 ROBERT STREET
87 FLASPOLLER HOUSE

4941 St. Charles

Built circa 1905, this Beaux Arts house is notable for its well-tended garden and its imposing circular front porch.

88 ORLEANS CLUB

5005 St. Charles

Originally built as a residence in 1868 by Col. William Wynne, as a wedding gift for his daughter, it was remodeled in 1907 by architect Emile Weil. The Orleans Club, a private ladies' organization, has been housed there since 1925.

At this time, reboard an Uptown-bound streetcar to continue the tour.

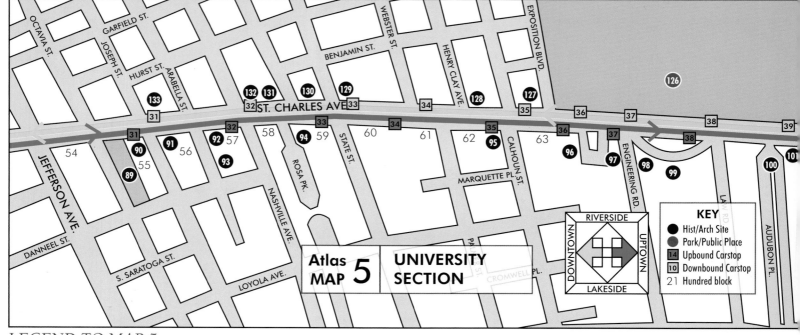

LEGEND TO MAP 5

CAR STOP 31
  Joseph Street
89 DANNEEL PARK
90 BENJAMIN HOUSE
  5531 St. Charles Avenue
91 McCARTHY HOUSE
  5603 St. Charles Avenue

92 TARA
  5705 St. Charles Avenue
93 JUDAH P. BENJAMIN'S COUNTRY HOUSE
  1630 Arabella Street
CAR STOP 32
  Nashville Avenue

94 WEDDING CAKE HOUSE
  5809 St. Charles Avenue
CAR STOP 35
  Calhoun Street
95 TEMPLE SINAI
  6227 St. Charles Avenue

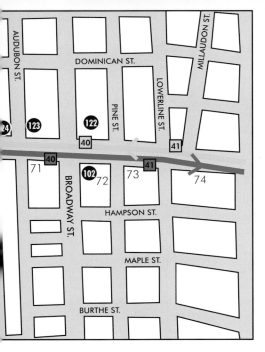

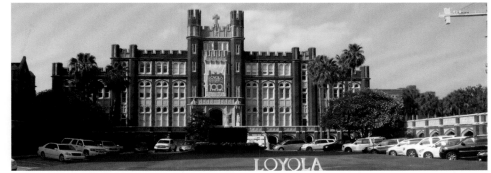

Loyola University, 1904

98 MIDDLE AMERICAN RESEARCH INSTITUTE
  Dinwiddie Hall, Tulane University
CAR STOP 38
99 TULANE UNIVERSITY
  6823 St. Charles Avenue
100 AUDUBON PLACE
  6800 St. Charles Avenue
CAR STOP 39
  Walnut Street
101 ZEMURRAY HOUSE
  2 Audubon Place
CAR STOP 40
  Broadway Street
102 DOLL HOUSE
  7209 St. Charles Avenue

Tulane University

Audubon Place

CAR STOP 36
  Exposition Boulevard
96 LOYOLA UNIVERSITY
  6363 St. Charles Avenue
CAR STOP 37
  Audubon Park
97 HOLY NAME OF JESUS CHURCH

45

CAR STOP 31 JOSEPH STREET
89 DANNEEL PARK
uptown lake corner of St. Charles and Octavia

This pleasant half-block neighborhood park is named for a New Orleans notable, Rudolph Danneel. He lived alone and his only pastime was writing poems and setting them to music. But he was rich and bequeathed the land to the city.

90 BENJAMIN HOUSE
5531 St. Charles

Built circa 1916 by Emile Weil for E. V. Benjamin, this Beaux Arts-style mansion, constructed of dressed limestone, an extremely costly material in New Orleans, is one of the most beautiful on St. Charles Avenue.

McCarthy House, 1903

91 McCARTHY HOUSE
5603 St. Charles

Designed in the style best described as Revived Greek Revival, very popular in the South in the early 20th century, this 1903 home is an outstanding example of its type.

92 TARA
5705 St. Charles

This is a replica of the home of Scarlett O'Hara in the movie *Gone With the Wind*. Tara, in the movie, was the creation of a set designer so this is truly life in imitation of art. It was built in 1941.

Wedding Cake House, 1896

CAR STOP 32 NASHVILLE AVENUE
94 THE WEDDING CAKE HOUSE
5809 St. Charles

The name of this house is rather misleading, as it was applied by a tour guide and has nothing to do with its architecture or its history. It is a splendid house designed by Toledano & Wogan and built in 1896 with all the Georgian Revival details popular at that time and some very elaborate garlands of flowers on the column capitals. The leaded beveled-glass front door may be the grandest in the city. It has been immortalized as the background for the etching of the St. Charles Streetcar by artist Philip Sage. It was also the background for a postcard of car 945 back in 1965.

CAR STOP 35 CALHOUN STREET
95 TEMPLE SINAI
6227 St. Charles

Organized in 1870 as the first Reform congregation in New Orleans, and located first near Lee Circle, the present building was constructed in 1928. The firm of Weiss, Dreyfous and Seiferth produced the unusual eclectic design. The addition at the corner of Palmer Avenue dates from 1970.

CAR STOP 36 EXPOSITION BOULEVARD
96 LOYOLA UNIVERSITY OF THE SOUTH
6363 St. Charles

This Roman Catholic institution is operated by the Society of Jesus, or the Jesuits, as the order is commonly known. Their influence in Louisiana began with Fr. Jacques Marquette, of the Marquette and Joliet expedition, which discovered and named the Mississippi River. Subsequently, the order purchased much of Bienville's Plantation until they were expelled from Louisiana in 1763. They returned in the 1840s and have been active in local education ever since.

The University was founded in 1904 and the campus contains 19 acres. The best-known schools are law, music, and communications.

The most impressive building is Marquette Hall, built in 1904, flanked on the downtown side by Thomas Hall and on the Uptown side by the Church of the Holy Name of Jesus. The architecture is a 20th-century blend of Gothic and Tudor.

Church of the Holy Name of Jesus, 1914

CAR STOP 37 AUDUBON PARK
97 CHURCH OF THE HOLY NAME OF JESUS

Built in 1914 by the same architects, DuBuys, Churchill, and LaBouisse, and of the same red brick as Marquette Hall. However, Holy Name is in a style that more accurately approximates Gothic. The interior is notable for its immense white marble high altar.

98 MIDDLE AMERICA RESEARCH INSTITUTE
Dinwiddie Hall

It has free pre-Columbian exhibits weekdays 9 a.m.-4 p.m.

CAR STOP 38 TULANE UNIVERSITY
99 TULANE UNIVERSITY
6823 St. Charles

Tulane University began in 1834 as the Medical College of Louisiana and became the University of Louisiana in 1847. However, the Louisiana government did not support the university, and in 1881 it received its largest single gift from Paul Tulane, a businessman and philanthropist from Princeton, N.J. who made most of his fortune here. Soon after, the campus moved from University Place in the Central Business District to this site. The oldest structure is Gibson Hall, the central building facing St. Charles Avenue, built in 1894 in the then popular Romanesque style. On the downtown side is Dinwiddie Hall, 1936, and on the uptown side is Tilton Hall, 1901, which has windows by Louis Comfort Tiffany.

Tulane is a leading institution of higher learning in the South, and together with the University of New Orleans, a state institution of much more recent date, contributes the predominant share of the city's academic reputation. The best-known school is still the Medical College.

100 AUDUBON PLACE
6800 St. Charles

Called Millionaires' Row by some, this is the only true private street in the city, complete with a chain and a guard to keep out unauthorized vehicles. The imposing gates were built in 1894 and development of the 28 building lots soon followed.

Zemurray House, 1907

CAR STOP 39 WALNUT STREET
101 ZEMURRAY HOUSE
2 Audubon Place

It is one of the more attractive homes on the street, located on the uptown corner of St. Charles Avenue. Built in 1907 for the Jay family, it was long the home of Samuel Zemurray, known as Sam the Banana Man, chairman of the United Fruit Company. He was a benefactor of Tulane and left his home as the residence of the university's president.

CAR STOP 40 BROADWAY STREET
102 DOLL HOUSE
7209 St. Charles

The main house is a good example of the Tudor Revival style, which had begun in England half a century earlier but arrived in New Orleans at the beginning of the 20th century. The remarkable thing here is the Tudor Revival doll house in the side yard.

Here you can transfer to the Leonidas bus line to get to the Audubon Zoo. Look for the bus stop sign on the uptown river corner of St. Charles and Broadway. Skip the next section if you stay on the streetcar.

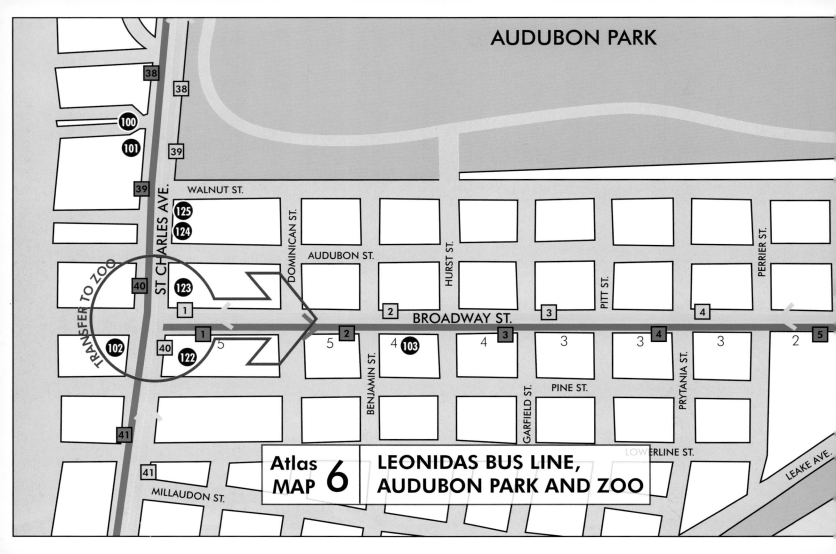

AUDUBON PARK

WALNUT ST.

ST CHARLES AVE.

TRANSFER TO ZOO

DOMINICAN ST.

AUDUBON ST.

HURST ST.

PERRIER ST.

PITT ST.

BENJAMIN ST.

GARFIELD ST.

PINE ST.

PRYTANIA ST.

BROADWAY ST.

LOWERLINE ST.

LEAKE AVE.

MILLAUDON ST.

Atlas MAP 6 **LEONIDAS BUS LINE, AUDUBON PARK AND ZOO**

38
38
100
101
39
39
125
124
40
123
1
102
40
122
41
41
1
5
2
2
5
103
4
4
3
3
3
4
3
3
2
5

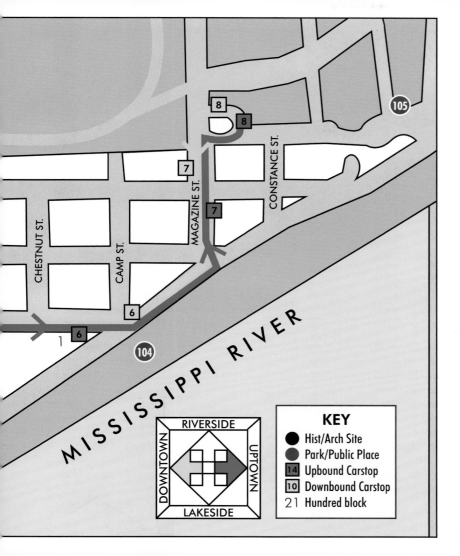

LEGEND TO MAP 6

BUS STOP 2
  Benjamin Street
103 GOGREVE HOUSE
  460 Broadway Street
BUS STOP 6
  corner Broadway Steet and Leake Avenue
104 MISSISSIPPI RIVER LEVEE
BUS STOP 8
  Magazine Street
105 AUDUBON PARK, AUDUBON ZOO

Levee

BUS STOP 6
104 LEVEE
corner of Broadway and Leake

The levee of the Mississippi River is one of the most interesting objects of the manmade environment. All levees by definition hold back floodwaters to protect cities and agricultural lands, but the river levee is part of a more complex function, which is a problem as well as a solution.

The natural environment of coastal Louisiana, of which New Orleans is a part, is composed of the delta of the Mississippi River. All of the land was created by the river over millions of years as it dropped its alluvial soil burden when reaching the Gulf of Mexico and during the annual spring floods. The river has changed course several times, creating a network of relatively high land.

Levees were raised to protect the settlements on the banks and ridges from floods and have become more sophisticated over the centuries of occupation. Today the levee system; spillways, which are really safety valves; and the flood-control structure at Old River, north of Baton Rouge, keep the river from changing course. The natural process of land creation has been disrupted, and the delta is subsiding and being lost to the Gulf of Mexico.

It was not until 1893 that a comprehensive drainage plan was initiated and completed in 1904. The system involves gravity flow from the river toward Lake Pontchartrain, but at one point it must be pumped part of that distance. The number of pumps and canals increased as the city grew, but some original 1904 equipment is still in use. Today there are 22 pumping stations, which have a combined capacity of more than 29 billion gallons in 24 hours. However, some spring rains overwhelm the system, which is designed to handle 1.5 inches the first hour of a storm and .5 inch thereafter.

BUS STOP 8 MAGAZINE STREET
105 AUDUBON PARK AND ZOOLOGICAL GARDENS

HISTORY

The site of Audubon Park has long been important in the activities of New Orleans. In 1795 it was part of the plantation of Etienne de Bore and his son-in-law, Pierre Foucher. This was the year that de Bore successfully granulated sugar for the first time and revolutionized the sugar industry, the Louisiana economy, and the diet of Western man.

Twice it was used as a military campground. Andrew Jackson rested here on his way to defend New Orleans in 1814. Later, during the occupation of New Orleans, Union troops were quartered on the land from 1862 to 1867.

In 1871, the Board of Park Commissioners of City Park, a state agency, was authorized to purchase additional land for public parks. This resulted in the purchase of a substantial part of the Foucher Plantation for a consideration that included assuming 27 notes, each valued at $27,000.

In 1884 the present park began to take shape. The name was changed to Audubon Park in honor of John James Audubon, the famous artist of the *Birds of America*. Audubon lived in Louisiana but where he was born is unknown.

That was also the year that the World's Industrial & Cotton Centennial Exposition opened in December. In addition to giving New Orleanians their first sight of an electric street railway, it gave the park a national reputation and created a wealth of legends and stories. A favorite among these legends recalls that the Japanese exhibitors introduced water hyacinths to Louisiana waterways, which now clog many navigable bayous and are the source of continuing controversy.

The Exposition was a source of some controversy itself. Despite having what was billed as, and probably was, the world's largest building, it closed in June 1885. An attempt to reopen in the fall of that year as the North, Central, and South American Exposition failed and was closed in April of 1886.

The park's governing body was changed in 1886, 1897, and 1914 with the creation of the Audubon Park Commission, which is still entrusted with its management and development.

THE PARK TODAY

Audubon Park with its spacious design by the famous landscape architect Frederick Law Olmstead is the major recreation area for Uptown. Casual observation suggests that its 3 greatest uses are golf, running, and the zoo, but there are many other things to see and do. Within its 340 acres one moves through open fields and live-oak alleys, from the urban activity of St. Charles Avenue and the University District to the levee of the Mississippi River. There the view opens to the awesome expanse of America's greatest waterway and her fourth largest port (in volume of containers handled) with ships of all sizes from around the world passing in review.

A visit to the park can easily entertain you for an entire day or more.

THINGS TO SEE

AUDUBON ZOOLOGICAL GARDENS
DIRECT ROUTE:
Get off at **BUS STOP 8** on the Leonidas line.
LEISURELY ROUTE:
Get off at **CAR STOPS 37, 38, OR 39**, cross to the river side of St. Charles Avenue, and walk into the park. You walk past the golf course and reach Magazine Street. The zoo is across Magazine on the Uptown side of the park.
DAYS AND HOURS:
Tue-Sun., 10 a.m.-5 p.m.
ADMISSION:
Adults $16, Children (2-12) $11, and Senior Citizens (65+)/Students $13.
INFORMATION:
1-800-774-7394

Return to St. Charles Avenue and board an Uptown-bound streetcar to continue the tour.

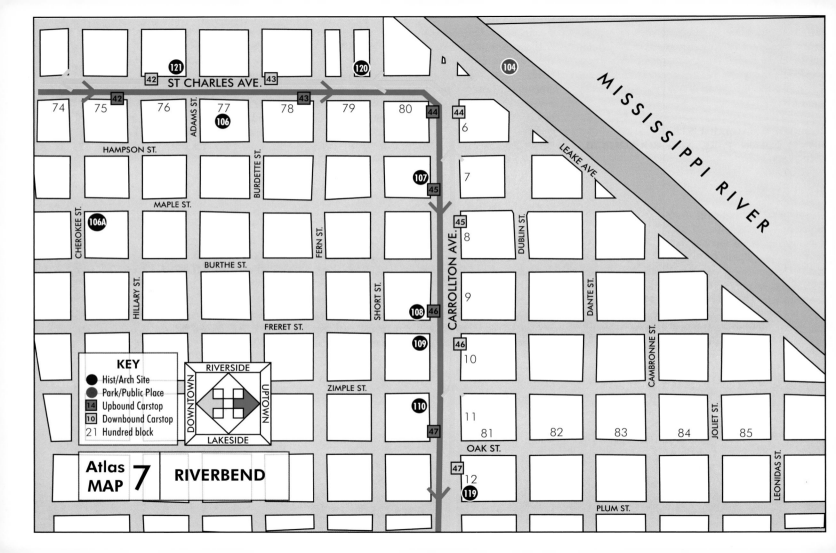

MISSISSIPPI RIVER

ST CHARLES AVE.

121
120
42
43
104

74 75 76 77 78 79 80
106
44
44
6

HAMPSON ST.

ADAMS ST.
BURDETTE ST.

107
45
7

MAPLE ST.

106A

FERN ST.

BURTHE ST.

CHEROKEE ST.
HILLARY ST.

LEAKE AVE.

DUBLIN ST.
45
8

SHORT ST.

9

DANTE ST.

108
46

FRERET ST.

CARROLLTON AVE.

109
46
10

ZIMPLE ST.

CAMBRONNE ST.

110
11
81 82 83 84 85

JOLIET ST.
LEONIDAS ST.

47

OAK ST.

47
12
119

PLUM ST.

KEY
● Hist/Arch Site
● Park/Public Place
14 Upbound Carstop
10 Downbound Carstop
21 Hundred block

RIVERSIDE
DOWNTOWN   UPTOWN
LAKESIDE

Atlas MAP **7** **RIVERBEND**

LEGEND TO MAP 7

CAR STOP 42
Hillary Street
106A MAPLE STREET BOOK SHOP
www.maplestreetbookshop.com
106 7717 ST. CHARLES AVENUE
CAR STOP 44
South Carrollton Avenue
RIVERBEND SHOPS
CAR STOP 45
Maple Street
107 AUDUBON CHARTER SCHOOL
719 S. Carrollton Avenue
MAPLE STREET SHOPS
CAR STOP 46
Freret Street
108 CARROLLTON UNITED
  METHODIST CHURCH
921 S. Carrollton Avenue
109 WILKINSON-DERBY HOUSE
1015 S. Carrollton Avenue
110 ST. ANDREW EPISCOPAL CHURCH
8017 Zimple Street
CAR STOP 47
OAK STREET SHOPS

CAR STOP 42 HILLARY STREET
106 7717 ST. CHARLES

One of the older of the large homes in Carrollton, it was built circa 1870 in a rather free combination of Italianate and Second Empire styles. The result is quite pleasing, although its cupola is partially hidden from view by trees. It is hard to see when you are going uptown on a streetcar, but you might catch a glimpse going back downtown.

CAR STOP 44 SOUTH CARROLLTON
RIVERBEND SHOPS

CAR STOP 45 MAPLE STREET
107 AUDUBON CHARTER SCHOOL
719 S. Carrollton

Built in 1854 as the Jefferson Parish Courthouse and designed by Henry Howard in the Greek Revival style, it has been a public school since the city of Carrollton was annexed to New Orleans. Jefferson Parish (same as a county) is our neighbor to the west. Parish lines were moved west when Carrollton became a part of New Orleans proper.

MAPLE STREET SHOPS

CAR STOP 46 FRERET STREET
108 CARROLLTON UNITED METHODIST CHURCH
921 S. Carrollton

Originally a German congregation organized in a private home, the church moved to the present site in 1886. The current church, with its outstanding red stone columns, was built in 1919.

109 WILKINSON-DERBY HOUSE
1015 S. Carrollton

Difficult to see behind its lush foliage, this Gothic Revival house, built circa 1849, is one of the oldest in the Carrollton area. It is interesting that this house and Briggs-Staub House in the Garden District (see map 3) are the only masonry Gothic Revival houses in the city, and both are of the same date.

110 ST. ANDREW EPISCOPAL CHURCH
8017 Zimple

Built in 1955 on the site of an older church (1903), the building is notable for the carvings over the S. Carrollton Avenue entrance front. The symbols of the Christian faith are depicted as heraldic devices.

CAR STOP 47 OAK STREET
OAK STREET SHOPS

This is the old neighborhood shopping center of Carrollton.

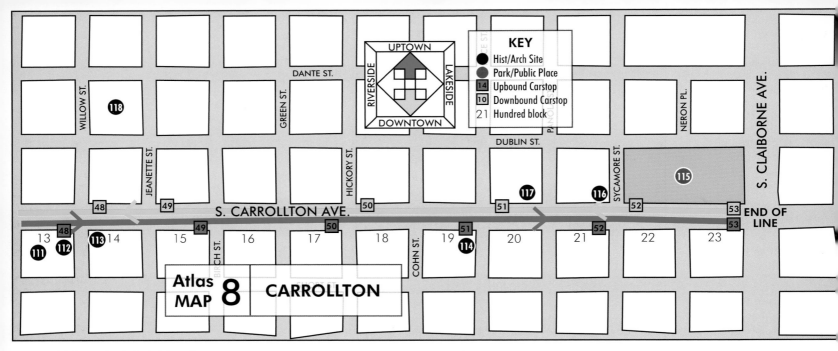

KEY
● Hist/Arch Site
● Park/Public Place
14 Upbound Carstop
10 Downbound Carstop
21 Hundred block

UPTOWN
RIVERSIDE   LAKESIDE
DOWNTOWN

WILLOW ST.
118

DANTE ST.
GREEN ST.

JEANETTE ST.
48   49

HICKORY ST.
50

DUBLIN ST.
51

SYCAMORE ST.
117   116   52   115   53   END OF LINE

NERON PL.
S. CLAIBORNE AVE.

S. CARROLLTON AVE.
48   49   50   51   52   53

13   48   14   15   49   16   17   50   18   19   51   20   21   52   22   23
111   112   113   BIRCH ST.   COHN ST.   114

Atlas MAP 8 CARROLLTON

LEGEND TO MAP 8

CAR STOP 48
  Willow Street
111 SULLY'S SECOND HOUSE
  1305 S. Carrollton Avenue
112 ST. MATTHEW UNITED CHURCH
  OF CHRIST
  1333 S. Carrollton Avenue

113 NIX LIBRARY
  1401 S. Carrollton Avenue.
CAR STOP 51
  Spruce Street
114 1939 S. CARROLLTON AVENUE
CAR STOP 53
  end of the line

115 PALMER PARK

CAR STOP 48 WILLOW STREET
111 SULLY'S SECOND HOUSE
1305 S. Carrollton

The second home designed by Thomas Sully for his own use (see 141 on map 4), it was completed in 1893. One of the earliest examples of the Colonial Revival in New Orleans, it was considered a reaction to the flamboyance of the Queen Anne style, which was Sully's earlier medium. An interesting detail is the circular stained-glass window picturing a naval pennant. Sully was Commodore of the Southern Yacht Club.

112 ST. MATTHEW UNITED CHURCH OF CHRIST
1333 S. Carrollton

The building was constructed in 1923, but the congregation, founded in 1849 as the German Evangelical Congregation of Carrollton, is the oldest Protestant ministry in Carrollton. The present name was taken upon the union of the Evangelical and Reformed Church with the Congregational Christian Church in 1957.

113 NIX PUBLIC LIBRARY
1401 S. Carrollton

A small neighborhood library built at the beginning of the 20th century, it is named for Dr. J. T. Nix, who, along with his brothers, donated the property in 1932.

CAR STOP 51 SPRUCE STREET
114 1939 S. CARROLLTON

This house, designed in an eclectic early-20th-century style, is quite remarkable. Certain characteristics could be called Art Deco, but as a whole, it is a unique and curious building.

CAR STOP 53 END OF THE LINE

This car stop is located at the intersection of S. Carrollton and S. Claiborne. Yes, you read this correctly—two intersecting streets marked south—but throw away your compass, as neither street runs due south. You may wish to photograph the street signs, as it may be one of the few points in the world where two streets marked south cross each other. This is due to the bend in the river. Carrollton is straight, while Claiborne twists and turns, following the curves of the Mississippi. It is here that the streetcars reverse direction and seats (interesting to watch), and you are asked to detrain and wait for this process before returning downtown. At this point, you will either have to use your pass again or come up with the full fare in order to return. But first, look to your left on the Uptown side of Carrollton.

115 PALMER PARK
S. Carrollton and S. Claiborne

In the original plan for Carrollton, this property was identified as Hamilton Square and has always been a public place. It was renamed Palmer Park in 1902, for Dr. Benjamin M. Palmer, a Presbyterian minister, at which time the entrance arch was erected.

The tour now reverses and returns to Canal Street. Car stops in this direction are now indicated in yellow on maps 8 through 1. Again, the sights are on your right as the car goes forward. Follow the yellow routes on maps 8 through 1.

LEGEND TO MAP 8

CAR STOP 52
Sycamore Street
116 BUNGALOID HOUSE
2140 S. Carrollton Avenue
117 CARROLLTON PRESBYTERIAN CHURCH
2032 S. Carrollton Avenue
CAR STOP 48
Willow Street
118 CARROLLTON CAR BARN
8201 Willow Street

Red bungaloid

CAR STOP 52 SYCAMORE STREET
116 RED BUNGALOID
2140 S. Carrollton

This house is a very good example of the domestic architecture of the 1920s. It is large and comfortable with porches and verandahs, much in the manner of Queen Anne homes built decades earlier, but in detail it is modern and of no identifiable style. Homes of this sort, called bungalows by their original developers, have come to be known as bungaloids by New Orleanians.

117 CARROLLTON PRESBYTERIAN CHURCH
2032 S. Carrollton

A 20th-century building of simple design reflecting a Mediterranean influence.

Carrollton car barn, 1893

CAR STOP 48 WILLOW STREET
118 CARROLLTON CAR BARN
8201 Willow

While not open to the public, this impressive structure dates back to 1893, when electric streetcars first appeared on St. Charles Avenue. The car barn is not only a storage facility but houses a large shop area capable of rebuilding our 1920s streetcars and actually building 30 heritage cars that run on the Canal and Riverfront lines.

LEGEND TO MAP 7

BEFORE CAR STOP 47
Oak Street
119 MATER DOLOROSA CHURCH
1228 S. Carrollton Avenue
CAR STOP 44
corner Carrollton and St. Charles avenues
104 MISSISSIPPI RIVER LEVEE
120 VICTORIAN COTTAGE
7922 St. Charles Avenue
CAR STOP 43
Burdette Street
121 CAMELBACKS
7632-34 and 7628-30 St. Charles Avenue

BEFORE CAR STOP 47 OAK STREET
119 MATER DOLOROSA CHURCH
1228 S. Carrollton

On the corner of Plum, this beautiful church was built in 1901. It is an interesting example of Renaissance Revival architecture and is the parish that serves the Carrollton area. Like many older areas of the city, Carrollton had both German- and English-speaking Roman Catholic congregations, but here they united to build a single monumental church.

CAR STOP 44 CARROLLTON AND ST. CHARLES
104 LEVEE

See page 50 for description.

120 VICTORIAN COTTAGE

7922 St. Charles

This gingerbread cottage of circa 1880 is a charming reminder of Carrollton in the days when it was a suburban town.

Camelbacks

CAR STOP 43 BURDETTE STREET
121 CAMELBACKS

7632-34 and 7628-30 St. Charles

These 2 cottages are examples of a characteristic style of local architecture especially popular in the second half of the 19th century. These probably date from the 1880s as 7628-30 still has the original gingerbread decoration popular then. The name comes from the fact that the front of the house has a single story and the rear has 2. This hump configuration was, according to one tale, created to avoid taxes that were levied on the height of the façade. It is also possible that it evolved from older buildings that were 1-story cottages with 2-story service wings.

LEGEND TO MAP 5

CAR STOP 40
Broadway Street
122 LOYOLA BROADWAY CAMPUS
7214 St. Charles Avenue
123 ST. CHARLES AVENUE BAPTIST CHURCH
7100 St. Charles Avenue
124 7030 ST. CHARLES AVENUE
125 7004 ST. CHARLES AVENUE
CAR STOP 38
126 AUDUBON PARK
CAR STOP 35
Calhoun Street
127 ROUND TABLE CLUB
6330 St. Charles Avenue
128 ST. CHARLES AVENUE CHRISTIAN CHURCH
6200 St. Charles Avenue
CAR STOP 33
State Street
129 CASTLE'S HOUSE
6000 St. Charles Avenue
130 ST. CHARLES AVENUE PRESBYTERIAN CHURCH
1545 State Street
131 PALACIO HOUSE
5824 St. Charles Avenue

CAR STOP 32
Nashville Avenue
132 HILLMAN HOUSE
5800 St. Charles Avenue
CAR STOP 31
Joseph Street
133 SISTER HOUSES
5624 and 5604 St. Charles Avenue

CAR STOP 40 BROADWAY
122 LOYOLA BROADWAY CAMPUS
7214 St. Charles

This was formerly St. Mary's Dominican College. The Dominican Sisters arrived in New Orleans in 1860 and opened a school for girls near Lee Circle. In 1864 a private school was placed at auction and the sisters bought it. It became a college in 1910. The oldest building on the campus faces St. Charles Avenue across a wide garden with many fine live oaks and palms. It was built in 1882 in a generally Italianate style.

123 ST. CHARLES AVENUE BAPTIST CHURCH
7100 St. Charles

The congregation was established from a mission of the Coliseum Place Baptist Church. Their first church was at the corner of St. Charles and Hillary. This building, in the Spanish Mission style, was constructed in 1926.

124 7030 ST. CHARLES AVENUE

Built circa 1880, the gingerbread Queen Anne-style house displays almost all the characteristics that are popularly termed Victorian. Notice the large metal cauldron in the front yard, which is an old sugar pot used in the granulation process in the 19th century.

125 7004 ST. CHARLES AVENUE
This large building is said to date from the 1890s and is in the style best described as Georgian Revival.

Audubon Park

CAR STOP 38 AUDUBON PARK ENTRANCE
126 AUDUBON PARK
In 1795 this land was the plantation of Etienne deBore who, in that year, developed a method of granulating sugar that was commercially successful and created the sugar industry in Louisiana.

In 1871 the land was purchased for public use but remained untouched until 1884 for the Cotton Centennial Exposition.

The park is named in honor of John James Audubon, the naturalist and artist, whose statue is in the zoo.

CAR STOP 35 CALHOUN STREET
127 ROUND TABLE CLUB
6330 St. Charles
Founded in the 19th century as a gentleman's club dedicated to good conversation and discussion of esoteric topics, the membership has included many artists and intellectuals. The club house is a fine Beaux Arts building with a magnificent stained-glass window on the downtown side. Today it is used as a reception hall.

128 ST. CHARLES AVENUE CHRISTIAN CHURCH
6200 St. Charles
This Colonial Revival building was dedicated in 1923. The congregation, organized in 1845, moved to this site in 1915.

CAR STOP 33 STATE STREET
129 CASTLE'S HOUSE
6000 St. Charles
This elegant home, built in 1895, is important for its contribution to the architecture of the University District. Designed by Thomas Sully, it is an example of Georgian influence popular in domestic architecture then. Many of its elements are true to the conventions of Georgian architecture.

130 ST CHARLES AVENUE PRESBYTERIAN CHURCH
1545 State
The congregation became independent of the First Presbyterian Church, formerly located on Lafayette Square, in 1920. The current building, in the Gothic style, was built in 1930.

131 PALACIO HOUSE
5824 St. Charles
Antonio Palacio, who moved to New Orleans from the Spanish city of Bilbao, had this home designed by Henry Howard in 1867. The house, secluded from the street by high plantings, is in the Italianate style.

CAR STOP 32 NASHVILLE AVENUE
132 HILLMAN HOUSE
5800 St. Charles
Built circa 1870, in the early Italianate of the time, it seems like a villa displaced from the Garden District.

CAR STOP 31 JOSEPH STREET
133 SISTER HOUSES
5624 and 5604 St. Charles
Locals call these the "Sister Houses." They were constructed in 1884, in the Second Empire style, as a speculative venture by Col. Robert E. Rivers. The lore says they were built as wedding presents for 2 sisters, but this is not true. Locals also call Freret's Folly (see 59 on map 3) and another row of single-story houses on Coliseum near Jackson sister houses because they are almost identical to each other, but stories have sprung up regarding the term. These 2 on St. Charles Avenue were originally identical, but modifications over the years have changed their appearance slightly.

LEGEND TO MAP 4

CAR STOP 30
Jefferson Avenue
134 JEWISH COMMUNITY CENTER
5342 St. Charles Avenue
CAR STOP 29A
Dufossat Street
135 MILTON H. LATTER LIBRARY
5120 St. Charles Avenue
CAR STOP 28
Robert Street
136 VACCARO HOUSE
5010 St. Charles Avenue
CAR STOP 27
Bordeaux Street
137 KROWER HOUSE
4630 St. Charles Avenue
CAR STOP 26
Cadiz Street
138 ST. GEORGE'S EPISCOPAL CHURCH
4600 St. Charles Avenue
139 SMITH HOUSE
4534 St. Charles Avenue
CAR STOP 25
Napoleon Avenue
140 TOURO SYNAGOGUE
4238 St. Charles Avenue
CAR STOP 23
Constantinople Street

141 SULLY'S HOUSE
4010 St. Charles Avenue
142 GRANT HOUSE
3932 St. Charles Avenue
143 RAYNE MEMORIAL METHODIST CHURCH
3900 St. Charles Avenue
CAR STOP 22
Peniston Street
144 UNITY TEMPLE
3722 St. Charles Avenue
CAR STOP 21
Foucher Street
145 TOURO INFIRMARY
1401 Foucher Street
CAR STOP 20
Louisiana Avenue
146 FRERET MANSION
1525 Louisiana Avenue

CAR STOP 30 JEFFERSON AVENUE
134 JEWISH COMMUNITY CENTER
5342 St. Charles

A recent addition to the Avenue, this building was completed in 1963, replacing the Jewish Home for Children designed by Thomas Sully in 1886.

Latter Library, 1907

CAR STOP 29A DUFOSSAT STREET
135 MILTON H. LATTER MEMORIAL LIBRARY
5120 St. Charles

Donated to the city in 1948 as a memorial to the donor's son killed on Okinawa, this Beaux Arts mansion occupies a full block and is surrounded by terraced lawns and live oaks.

Built in 1907 by the Issacs family who owned a downtown department store, it was sold in 1912 to Frank B. Williams, the Louisiana lumber king. His son, Harry, a pioneer aviator, married Marguerite Clark, a silent-film star, and they lived in the home from her retirement until 1940.

The interiors of the reception rooms are still decorated as they were when it was a home. Particularly notable are the ceilings in the rooms on either side of the entrance, which have paintings dated circa 1858 that are said to be from Paris.

Vaccaro House, 1910

CAR STOP 28 ROBERT STREET
136 VACCARO HOUSE
5010 St. Charles

Built in 1910, this imposing house in the then newly popular Tudor style was designed for Joseph Vaccaro, who made his fortune importing bananas.

CAR STOP 27 BORDEAUX STREET
137 KROWER HOUSE
4630 St. Charles

Designed 1906 by Emile Weil, it is one of the few houses in the city with a basement partly below ground. This type of construction is rare in the city because of the high water table but was used in homes of this period as a way to incorporate the service area into the main house.

CAR STOP 26 CADIZ STREET
138 ST. GEORGE'S EPISCOPAL CHURCH
4600 St. Charles

Completed in 1900 in the Romanesque style, but in brick rather than stone, it was a symbol of the growth of the neighborhood.

139 SMITH HOUSE
4534 St. Charles

Built in 1906, this large home shows the Romanesque influence popular at the time in its column capitals and rough-hewn stone.

CAR STOP 25 NAPOLEON AVENUE

As you cross Napoleon Avenue on the streetcar, look toward the river. You will see a beautiful avenue lined with live oaks and crepe myrtles in the neutral ground. The Gothic spire of St. Stephen's Church, the tallest in New Orleans, will be visible towering over the avenue.

Napoleon Avenue is the main street of Bouligny. The street-name theme of this area was tied to Napoleon Bonaparte. Except for Berlin Street, changed to General Pershing during World War I, the 5 streets on each side of Napoleon Avenue are all named for cities associated with Napoleon's career.

140 TOURO SYNAGOGUE
4238 St. Charles

It was built in 1908 by architect Emile Weil, who was known locally for mansions and theatres in the Beaux Arts style. It is named for Judah Touro, the son of a Rhode Island rabbi. Touro was a local civic leader who, in his youth, was wounded in the Battle of New Orleans. In later life, his philanthropic efforts ranged from founding Touro Infirmary to finishing the Bunker Hill Monument in Boston.

CAR STOP 23 CONSTANTINOPLE STREET
141 SULLY'S HOUSE
4010 St. Charles

It was built circa 1890 by architect Thomas Sully for his family. It remains a well-preserved example of his work. You have already seen another of his homes, Sully's Second House on S. Carrollton Avenue (see 111 on map 8), described earlier.

142 GRANT HOUSE
3932 St. Charles

From Napoleon to Louisiana avenues, St. Charles Avenue was developed primarily from 1875 to 1890. Many of the mansions built here were designed by New Orleans architect Thomas Sully, who was a proponent of the eclectic style known as Queen Anne. This house, built in 1887, is probably his work and is representative of the style.

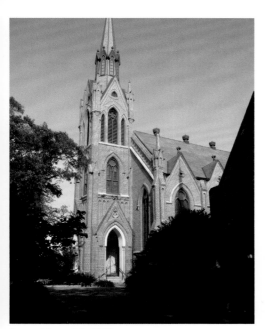
Rayne Memorial, 1875

143 RAYNE MEMORIAL UNITED METHODIST CHURCH
3900 St. Charles

Built in 1875 in memory of the donor's son, William Rayne, a casualty of the Battle of Chancellorsville, it is the oldest Methodist church building in the city. The simple but elegant Gothic spire is illuminated at night to serve as a continuing memorial.

CAR STOP 22 PENISTON STREET
144 UNITY TEMPLE
3722 St. Charles

Designed by a student of Frank Lloyd Wright, this unusual circular church was built in 1960.

CAR STOP 21 FOUCHER STREET
145 TOURO INFIRMARY
1401 Foucher

This hospital, now housed in a complex of mirrored high-rise buildings, is one of the oldest and largest in the city. Founded by Judah Touro in 1852, it was originally located in a home of the 1820s built near the river in the Coliseum Square area. The hospital moved to its present site in 1882.

Freret Mansion, circa 1850

CAR STOP 20 LOUISIANA AVENUE
146 FRERET MANSION
1525 Louisiana

Look to your right on the downtown side of Louisiana Avenue. In the middle of the block, behind the supermarket facing St. Charles, you will see Freret Mansion. Architect William A. Freret, the older brother of James Freret, built this Greek Revival home for his family in the early 1850s. Only occupied by 3 families, the house was the home of newspaper editor James Thompson and his wife, Genevieve, the daughter of Champ Clark, U.S. Speaker of the House in the early 20th century. Miss Clark was a friend of Alice Roosevelt (daughter of Teddy Roosevelt), who accompanied her to New Orleans.

LEGEND TO MAP 3

CARS STOP 17
Washington Avenue
147 BELFORT MANSION
2618 St. Charles Avenue

CAR STOP 17 WASHINGTON AVENUE
147 BELFORT MANSION
2618 St. Charles

The earliest record of this huge Greek Revival house is 1874. Most would recognize the mansion from MTV's "Real World" reality show. The house was restored back to a single-family residence in early 2005.

LEGEND TO MAP 1

CAR STOP 56 GIROD STREET
148 SCOTTISH RITE TEMPLE
619 Carondelet

Originally built in 1853 as a Methodist church, it was rededicated in 1906. The architectural changes included the removal of the tower, which was said to be a copy of the monument to Lysicrates in ancient Greece, and filling in the main door with a stained-glass panel. Nevertheless, it remains a major Greek Revival building.

CAR STOP 57 POYDRAS STREET
VISTA OF POYDRAS STREET TO LAKE

On the left, there is an opportunity to see the Mercedes-Benz Superdome, home of the Super Bowl 44 Champion New Orleans Saints.

149 FACTORS' ROW
802-22 Perdido

Built in 1858, it is an excellent example of mid-19th-century commercial buildings, restored and still occupied as offices. It was here, in the cotton-factoring office, that Edgar Degas painted the *Cotton Exchange*, which is now displayed in the Museum of Pau, France.

In the next 4 blocks to Canal Street you pass many of the buildings built in the early 20th century before technology permitted structures as tall as One Shell Square.

CAR STOP 58 GRAVIER STREET
150 HIBERNIA NATIONAL BANK BUILDING
307 Carondelet

Once the tallest building in the city, it is still a commanding structure topped by a fine Greek peristyle that is illuminated every night: purple, green, and gold during Mardi Gras; green on St. Patrick's Day, etc.

151 AMERICAN BANK BUILDING
200 Carondelet

Dedicated to its depositors in that inauspicious year of 1929, it was designed in the Art Deco style. Its fanciful cupola is a fine counterpart to the peristyle a block away.

CAR STOP 59 CANAL STREET
END OF THE LINE

Everyone must alight at this point. Please use the rear door to accommodate those getting on to go Uptown. Hope you enjoyed the Grand Tour of the Queen of New Orleans avenues, St. Charles Avenue!

Hibernia National Bank Building

CANAL STREETCAR TOUR

On the Canal Streetcar line, you have 2 options: Canal to the Cemeteries or Canal to City Park/New Orleans Museum of Art (NOMA). Beginning at car stop 1, at Canal near the mighty Mississippi River, the Cemeteries streetcar goes to City Park Avenue, at car stop 29. It is appropriately marked CANAL/ CEMETERIES. However, do not board a Cemeteries streetcar if you wish to go to City Park itself. Look for one marked CANAL/CARROLLTON, CANAL/ CITY PARK MUSEUM, or CANAL/CITY PARK instead. Those streetcars turn onto N. Carrollton and end 2 miles later at Beauregard Circle. This is the entrance to City Park, with NOMA accessible by a short walk in the park.

The route from the river to the Cemeteries runs approximately 3.5 miles. Cars stop at nearly every corner downtown, then every 2 blocks. Here is a helpful hint: Canal streetcars board toward traffic in the CBD, but past Claiborne Avenue, one gets on and off away from traffic, or toward the neutral ground.

We will begin with the Cemeteries route, from the foot of Canal Street (by the Mississippi River). Similar to the St. Charles tour, the outbound or lakebound route will be in blue on the maps, and the inbound or riverbound route will be in yellow.

MAPS

Map 9—Central Business District
Map 10—Broad Street to Pierce Street
Map 11—Pierce Street to Cemeteries
Map 12—North Carrollton Avenue/City Park
Map 13—Broad Street University Hospital Area to Claiborne Avenue

LEGEND TO MAP 9

CAR STOP 1
foot of Canal Street
1 ALGIERS/GRETNA FERRIES
2 SPANISH PLAZA
1 Poydras Street
3 AUDUBON AQUARIUM OF THE AMERICAS
1 Canal Street
CAR STOP 2
North Peters Street
4 CANAL PLACE SHOPPING MALL
333 Canal Street
5 U.S. CUSTOMS HOUSE/AUDUBON INSECTARIUM
423 Canal Street
CAR STOP 4
Chartres Street
6 MARRIOTT HOTEL
555 Canal Street
7 WERLEIN'S MUSIC BUILDING
605 Canal Street
CAR STOP 5
ROYAL STREET
CAR STOP 6
BOURBON STREET
8 D. H. HOLMES BUILDING
819 Canal Street

CAR STOP 7
Dauphine Street
9 MAISON BLANCHE BUILDING
921 Canal Street
10 AUDUBON BUILDING
929 Canal Street
CAR STOP 8
North Rampart Street
11 SAENGER THEATRE
143 North Rampart Street
12 SIMON BOLIVAR STATUE
13 VISTA TO ST. LOUIS CEMETERY NO. 1
501 Basin Street
CAR STOP 10
Marais Street
14 TEXACO BUILDING
1501 Canal Street
15 VISTA TO ST. LOUIS CEMETERY NO. 2
720 Conti Street
CAR STOP 11
North Claiborne Avenue

Maison Blanche Building, 1908

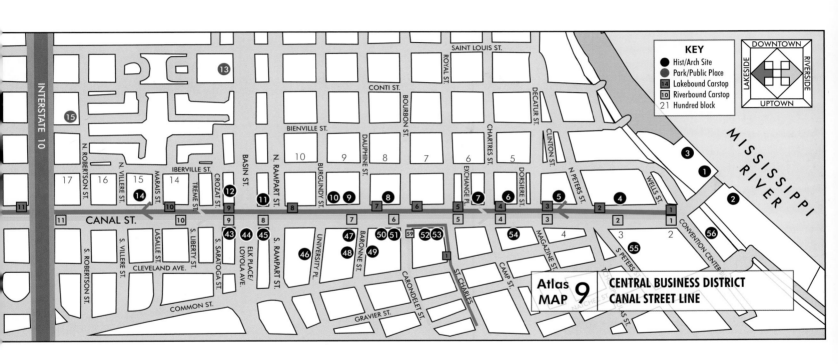

Atlas MAP 9 CENTRAL BUSINESS DISTRICT CANAL STREET LINE

CAR STOP 1 FOOT OF CANAL
1 ALGIERS/GRETNA FERRIES

There are great views of our Central Business District and the French Quarter if you take the ferryboat to Algiers, free to pedestrians and a charge of $1 per car for the return trip to the east bank. This is another point in the city where your compass does you no good whatsoever. Because of the crescent-shaped bends in the river, it flows due north at Canal Street, and the sun rises over the west bank and sets over the east bank. Really! The ferry ride to Algiers is very short. You can make a round trip in a half-hour, or stroll around Algiers Point if you have the time. The other boat going to Gretna (pedestrian only) is great if you have more time and want to see more of the river up close. The Gretna Ferry departure times vary depending on the day of the week, but it basically leaves Canal Street every hour.

2 SPANISH PLAZA
1 Poydras

The Spanish Plaza was dedicated in 1976 to the city of New Orleans by Spain in tribute to our common history. Note the seals of the Spanish provinces surrounding the fountain.

3 AUDUBON AQUARIUM OF THE AMERICAS
1 Canal Street

Featuring a walk-through tunnel of a Caribbean coral reef, the Aquarium of the Americas is a wonderful, worthwhile destination.

Board the streetcar in the middle of Canal Street. You are now on an outbound, or lakebound, car.

As a side note, it is here at Canal and Wells Street where Blanche DuBois got off an L&N train and boarded a "Streetcar Named Desire" in the 1951 movie of the same name. See car stop 11 Rampart Street for more on this.

CAR STOP 2 NORTH PETERS STREET
4 CANAL PLACE SHOPPING MALL
333 Canal

This is an upscale shopping mall.

As you head up Canal, streets marked *south* are to your left, *north* to the right. South at this point actually runs southwest, and that is Uptown New Orleans.

5 U.S. CUSTOMS HOUSE/ AUDUBON INSECTARIUM
423 Canal

The Customs House dates back to 1881, although its construction began in 1848. The interruption was due to the Civil War. The building was declared a National Historic Landmark in 1974. The exterior of the Customs House retains its original design, which includes modified Greek and Egyptian Revival elements and is known for its Egyptian Revival columns.

CAR STOP 4 CHARTRES STREET
6 MARRIOTT HOTEL
555 Canal

Werlein's Music Building

7 WERLEIN'S MUSIC BUILDING
605 Canal

If you grew up in New Orleans, either you or someone you know bought musical equipment and/or took lessons at Werlein's. A New Orleans institution since 1853, the business was sold in 1940 to David Franck and remained open until the early 2000s. This impressive building now houses an upscale restaurant.

CAR STOP 5 ROYAL STREET

Royal Street becomes St. Charles. However, ride 1 more block up Canal to Bourbon/Carondelet to get the St. Charles Streetcar.

CAR STOP 6 BOURBON STREET

World-famous Bourbon Street becomes Carondelet on the American side, and it is here, on the uptown-river corner, that you can change to one of our Perley Thomas streetcars for a ride up St. Charles Avenue.

8 D. H. HOLMES BUILDING
819 Canal

Originally a New Orleans-based department store founded in 1842 by Daniel Henry Holmes, the franchise was sold to Dillard's in 1989. Every New Orleanian is familiar with the famous "Holmes Clock," which is still there although partially hidden. It was featured in the book *Confederacy of Dunces*, when Ignatius Reilly meets his mom there. The iconic building is now in use as the Chateau Bourbon Hotel.

CAR STOP 7 DAUPHINE STREET
9 MAISON BLANCHE BUILDING
921 Canal

Maison Blanche, which is French for "white house," is a distinctive structure built in 1908. By the mid-20th century, the upper floors were occupied by medical and dental offices, but they basically emptied out by the 1990s. In 1997, work began to use the lower floors for the Maison Blanche department store and the upper floors for part of a new Ritz-Carlton hotel. Now the whole building, along with the neighboring one, is part of the Ritz-Carlton, which had its grand opening in October of 2000.

10 AUDUBON BUILDING
929 Canal

Originally a hotel built in 1909, it was converted to office and retail space and used as such until 2004. Now it is a hotel again; the Saint opened in August of 2011.

CAR STOP 8 NORTH RAMPART STREET
11 SAENGER THEATRE
143 North Rampart

Opened on February 4, 1927, the Saenger Theatre is 1 of 4 in the immediate area around Canal and Rampart streets. Flooding from Hurricane Katrina closed the Saenger in August 2005. Renovations are expected to be completed in 2013.

FUTURE DESIRE STREETCAR LINE

Plans are in place to return streetcars to North Rampart, heading into the Marigny area and returning to make a loop around the French Quarter, similar to the old Desire line. Once this is opened, you could almost retrace Blanche's route from *A Streetcar Named Desire,* by getting on a Cemeteries car and transferring to Desire to get to Elysian Fields and Royal Street.

12 SIMON BOLIVAR STATUE

In the neutral ground of Basin Street is a statue of Simon Bolivar, dedicated in 1957 after the demolition of the Southern Railway Train station at this location. You will be able to transfer at this stop to the new Loyola Avenue Streetcar line, which will take you from Canal Street to the Union Passenger Terminal.

13 VISTA TO ST. LOUIS CEMETERY NO. 1
501 Basin

Here there is a vista to St. Louis Cemetery No. 1, well known for its occupants.

Between car stops 9 and 10 is Treme Street, famous from the HBO series "Treme." However, the term Treme refers to an area of town and not just the street.

CAR STOP 10 MARAIS STREET
14 TEXACO BUILDING
1501 Canal

On the downtown-lake corner is Canal Street's first skyscraper, the Texaco Building, built in the mid-19th century. It now serves as an assisted-living apartment complex. Also in the immediate area between Marais Street and Claiborne Avenue are Tulane and University of New Orleans satellite campuses.

15 VISTA TO ST. LOUIS CEMETERY NO. 2
720 Conti

Looking to your right around North Robertson Street, you can see St. Louis Cemetery No. 2. However, a walking tour of St. Louis No. 1 on Basin Street, St. Louis No. 3 on Esplanade Avenue, or Lafayette Cemetery in the Garden District would be recommended above this one.

CAR STOP 11 NORTH CLAIBORNE

I-10 runs overhead.

LEGEND TO MAP 10

CAR STOP 17
North White Street

16 NORTA FACILITY
2800-2900 blocks Canal Street

CAR STOP 18
North Salcedo Street

17 WARREN EASTON HIGH SCHOOL
3019 Canal Street

CAR STOP 20
North Jefferson Davis Parkway

**18 CANAL STREET UNITED
METHODIST CHURCH**
3401 Canal Street

CAR STOP 23
North Scott Street

19 SCHOEN FUNERAL HOME
3827 Canal Street

20 ST. JOHN'S LUTHERAN CHURCH
3937 Canal Street

Canal Street United Methodist Church, 1960

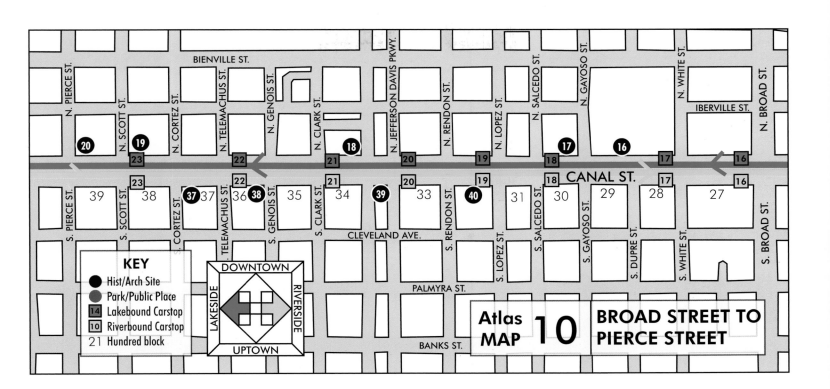

BIENVILLE ST.

N. PIERCE ST.
N. SCOTT ST.
N. CORTEZ ST.
N. TELEMACHUS ST.
N. GENOIS ST.
N. CLARK ST.
N. JEFFERSON DAVIS PKWY.
N. RENDON ST.
N. LOPEZ ST.
N. SALCEDO ST.
N. GAYOSO ST.
N. WHITE ST.
N. BROAD ST.

IBERVILLE ST.

20 **19** **18** **17** **16**

23 22 21 20 19 18 17 16

CANAL ST.

23 22 21 20 19 **18** 17 16

S. PIERCE ST.
S. SCOTT ST.
S. CORTEZ ST.
S. TELEMACHUS ST.
S. GENOIS ST.
S. CLARK ST.
S. RENDON ST.
S. LOPEZ ST.
S. SALCEDO ST.
S. GAYOSO ST.
S. DUPRE ST.
S. WHITE ST.
S. BROAD ST.

39 38 **37** 37 36 **38** 35 34 **39** 33 **40** 31 30 29 28 27

CLEVELAND AVE.

PALMYRA ST.

KEY
- ● Hist/Arch Site
- ● Park/Public Place
- 14 Lakebound Carstop
- 10 Riverbound Carstop
- 21 Hundred block

DOWNTOWN
LAKESIDE   RIVERSIDE
UPTOWN

BANKS ST.

Atlas **MAP 10**

BROAD STREET TO PIERCE STREET

Schoen Funeral Home

CAR STOP 17 NORTH WHITE STREET
16 NORTA FACILITY
2800-2900 blocks Canal

This location, which has been in use since 1861, houses our red cars overnight for storage and maintenance. The archways over the rear storage tracks are from the old Canal Barn.

CAR STOP 18 NORTH SALCEDO STREET
17 WARREN EASTON HIGH SCHOOL
3019 Canal

Opened in 1913 as a boys' school, it became coed in 1952. Today it is well known as the recipient of a large donation from actress Sandra Bullock.

CAR STOP 20 NORTH JEFFERSON DAVIS PARKWAY
18 CANAL STREET UNITED METHODIST CHURCH
3401 Canal

A relatively new landmark for Canal Street, this church was completed in 1960, though the congregation dates back to 1824.

CAR STOP 23 NORTH SCOTT STREET
19 SCHOEN FUNERAL HOME
3827 Canal

Once a large Eastlake-type house, it was converted to a funeral parlor in 1935, remodeled in the Spanish eclectic style.

20 ST. JOHN'S LUTHERAN CHURCH
3937 Canal

A part of New Orleans history since before the Civil War, the current congregation settled in this Mid-City location in 1924.

LEGEND TO MAP 11

CAR STOP 24
North Carrollton Avenue
CARROLLTON AVENUE SPUR
CAR STOP 27
North St. Patrick Street
21 THURGOOD MARSHALL PUBLIC SCHOOL
4625 Canal Street
CAR STOP 28
North Anthony Street
22 HOPE MAUSOLEUM
4841 Canal Street
22B BEACHCORNER BAR & GRILL
www.beachcornerbarandgrill.com
CAR STOP 29
City Park Avenue
23A THE HERB IMPORT COMPANY
www.herbimport.com
23 ODD FELLOWS REST CEMETERY
5055 Canal Street
24 GREENWOOD CEMETERY
5200 Canal Boulevard
25 CYPRESS GROVE CEMETERY
120 City Park Avenue
26 CHARITY HOSPITAL CEMETERY/ KATRINA MEMORIAL
5056 Canal Street

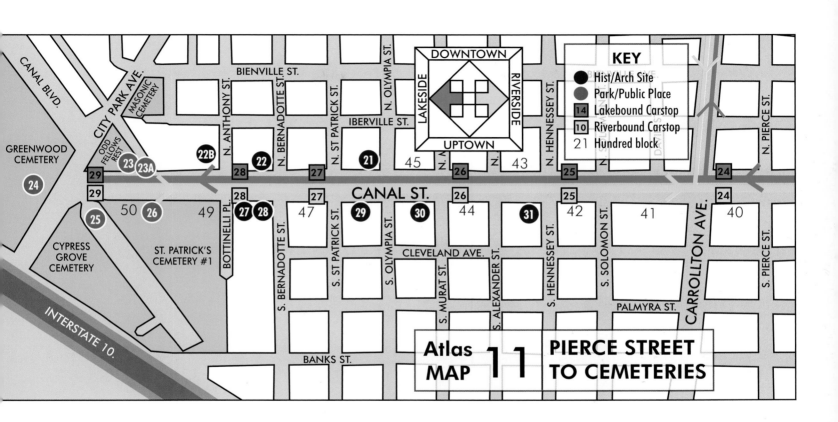

KEY

- ● Hist/Arch Site
- ● Park/Public Place
- 14 Lakebound Carstop
- 10 Riverbound Carstop
- 21 Hundred block

Atlas MAP **11** PIERCE STREET TO CEMETERIES

CAR STOP 24 NORTH CARROLLTON AVENUE
CARROLLTON AVENUE SPUR

The City Park streetcar turns here if it is marked CANAL/CARROLLTON, CANAL/CITY PARK MUSEUM, or CANAL/CITY PARK. However, our current tour continues to the Cemeteries. Skip to map 12 if you are on a Carrollton car. There are many good restaurants in this immediate area.

CAR STOP 27 NORTH ST. PATRICK STREET
21 THURGOOD MARSHALL PUBLIC SCHOOL
4625 Canal

It is a public college-preparatory high school operated in association with the University of New Orleans.

CAR STOP 28 NORTH ANTHONY STREET
22 HOPE MAUSOLEUM
4841 Canal

It was designed by Albert R. Huber and built in 1931. Mr. Huber studied mausoleum architecture at Columbia University.

CAR STOP 29 CITY PARK AVENUE
23 ODD FELLOWS REST CEMETERY
5055 Canal

New Orleans cemeteries are unlike any others nationwide. The tombs are above ground because of the high water table. They also appear to be, due to the concentration of them, cities of the dead. This type of interment reflects Louisiana's Spanish heritage.

24 GREENWOOD CEMETERY
5200 Canal Boulevard

25 CYPRESS GROVE CEMETERY
120 City Park

26 CHARITY HOSPITAL CEMETERY/
KATRINA MEMORIAL
5056 Canal Street

The tour now returns toward the river/CBD. The streetcar motorman moves to the other end of the car and reverses the seats, just as is done at the end of the St. Charles line. It is interesting to watch the process.

Car stops in this direction are now indicated in yellow on map 11. Again, the sights are on your right as the car goes forward. Follow the yellow route on map 11.

Jewish Cemetery

LEGEND TO MAP 11

CAR STOP 28
Bottinelli Place
27 JEWISH CEMETERY
4824 Canal Street
28 MCMAHON FUNERAL HOME BUILDING
4800 Canal Street
CAR STOP 27
South St. Patrick Street
29 ST. ANTHONY OF PADUA CATHOLIC CHURCH
4640 Canal Street
CAR STOP 26
South Murat Street
30 CENTANNI HOUSE
4506 Canal Street
CAR STOP 25
South Hennessey Street
31 CANAL STREET PRESBYTERIAN CHURCH
4302 Canal Street
CAR STOP 24
South Carrollton Avenue
CARROLLTON AVENUE SPUR

CAR STOP 28 BOTTINELLI PLACE
27 JEWISH CEMETERY
4824 Canal

McMahon Funeral Home Building, 1872

28 McMAHON FUNERAL HOME BUILDING
4800 Canal

Of course, with so many cemeteries nearby, there were many funeral parlors in this area, as this magnificent structure used to be. Built in 1872, it remained a funeral parlor until 2003. It is now a haunted-house Halloween attraction.

CAR STOP 27 SOUTH ST. PATRICK STREET
29 ST. ANTHONY OF PADUA CATHOLIC CHURCH
4640 Canal Street

While this parish dates back to 1915, it is not known when this beautiful church was built.

Centanni House, 1917

CAR STOP 26 SOUTH MURAT STREET
30 CENTANNI HOUSE
4506 Canal Street

On the uptown-lake corner is a property known to older New Orleanians as the "Centanni House." It was overwhelmingly popular in the 1950s and 1960s for its wonderful Christmas decorations. Built in 1917, this Craftsman-style bungalow is on the National Register of Historic Places.

CAR STOP 25 SOUTH HENNESSEY STREET
31 CANAL STREET PRESBYTERIAN CHURCH
4302 Canal

The present-day church was erected in 1927, but the congregation dates back to 1847.

CAR STOP 24 SOUTH CARROLLTON AVENUE
CARROLLTON AVENUE SPUR

At this point in the tour, we get off and take a City Park streetcar. If you wish to stay on the Canal Street tour, go to map 10.

LEGEND TO MAP 12

CAR STOP 25B
  Bienville Street
**32A ANGELO BROCATO ITALIAN ICE
  CREAM & PASTRIES**
  www.AngeloBrocatoicecream.com
CAR STOP 26B
  St. Louis Street
CAR STOP 29B
  City Park
32 BEAUREGARD CIRCLE
33 NEW ORLEANS CITY PARK
34 ENTRANCE TO CITY PARK
35 NEW ORLEANS MUSEUM OF ART
  1 Collins Diboll Circle
36 ST. LOUIS CEMETERY NO. 3
  3421 Esplanade Avenue
37 PITOT HOUSE
  1440 Moss Street

New Orleans Museum of Art, 1911

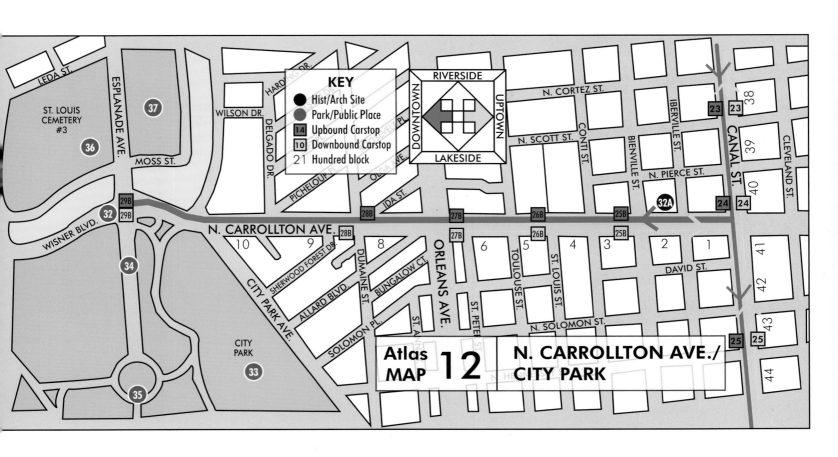

KEY

● Hist/Arch Site
● Park/Public Place
■ 14 Upbound Carstop
□ 10 Downbound Carstop
21 Hundred block

RIVERSIDE
DOWNTOWN
UPTOWN
LAKESIDE

ST. LOUIS CEMETERY #3

LEDA ST.
ESPLANADE AVE.
WILSON DR.
HARDING DR.
DELGADO DR.
MOSS ST.
PICHELOUP PL.
OLGA ST.
IDA ST.

WISNER BLVD.

N. CARROLLTON AVE.

CITY PARK AVE.

SHERWOOD FOREST DR.
DUMAINE ST.
ALLARD BLVD.
BUNGALOW CT.
SOLOMON PL.

ST. ANN ST.

ORLEANS AVE.

ST. PETER ST.

TOULOUSE ST.

ST. LOUIS ST.

N. SOLOMON ST.

N. HOLLY ST.

DAVID ST.

N. CORTEZ ST.
N. SCOTT ST.
CONTI ST.
N. PIERCE ST.
BIENVILLE ST.
IBERVILLE ST.
CANAL ST.
CLEVELAND ST.

CITY PARK

Atlas MAP 12   **N. CARROLLTON AVE./ CITY PARK**

36 37

32 29B 29B
28B
27B 26B 25B
32A
24 24
23 23 38
39
40
25 25
41 42 43 44

34
35
33

10 9 8 27B 6 5 4 3 2 1

CAR STOP 26B
ST. LOUIS STREET

If you have already been to our beloved French Quarter and paid some attention to the street names, you will notice they are the same here in the Mid-City area. Like Canal Street, most run from the river to City Park Avenue.

Beauregard statue

CAR STOP 29B CITY PARK
32 BEAUREGARD CIRCLE

As soon as you get off the streetcar, straight ahead is a statue of Civil War general P. G. T. Beauregard. The monument by Alexander Doyle depicts Beauregard on his horse, which has one foot raised, meaning the general was wounded in battle but survived.

33 NEW ORLEANS CITY PARK

Founded in 1853, New Orleans City Park has more than 1,300 acres, making it the 6th largest municipal park in the United States and almost double the size of Central Park in New York City.

Entrance to City Park

34 ENTRANCE TO CITY PARK

An extension of Esplanade Avenue, Lelong Drive is a grand entranceway to City Park and the New Orleans Museum of Art.

35 NEW ORLEANS MUSEUM OF ART
1 Collins Diboll Circle

The New Orleans Museum of Art (NOMA) is New Orleans' oldest fine-arts institution, opened in December 1911. It houses an impressive permanent collection of almost 40,000 objects.

St. Louis Cemetery No. 3, 1854

36 ST. LOUIS CEMETERY NO. 3
3421 Esplanade

Founded in 1854, this cemetery has more elaborate crypts than most, and it also has a Greek Orthodox section.

37 PITOT HOUSE
1440 Moss

This landmark is not visible from the City Park streetcar but is worth the short walk down Bayou St. John. Built in 1799, this Creole colonial plantation home is owned by the Louisiana Landmarks Society, which bought the house in 1960 and moved it to its current location to avoid demolition. It is named for James Pitot, New Orleans' first real mayor after the city's incorporation, who lived here from 1810 to 1819.

Reboard the streetcar to return to Canal Street (all streetcars leaving Beauregard Circle go downtown only, not to the Cemeteries). Heading riverbound, car stops on Canal Street are now indicated in yellow on map 10. Again, the sights are on your right as the car goes forward. Follow the yellow route on map 10.

LEGEND TO MAP 10

CAR STOP 22
South Telemachus Street
37 GRACE EPISCOPAL CHURCH
3700 Canal Street
38 BLOCK KELLER HOUSE
3620 Canal Street
CAR STOP 20
South Jefferson Davis Parkway
39 STATUE OF JEFFERSON DAVIS
CAR STOP 19
South Lopez Street
40 SACRED HEART CATHOLIC CHURCH
3200 Canal Street

CAR STOP 22 SOUTH TELEMACHUS STREET
37 GRACE EPISCOPAL CHURCH
3700 Canal

The growing pains of this parish, one of the older Episcopal congregations in South Louisiana, caused it to build a newer church. The old church was on the site of the Texaco Building (see map 9). The present building was completed in 1954.

38 BLOCK KELLER HOUSE
3620 Canal

The Block Keller House is a 1912 neoclassical villa, now used as a bed and breakfast.

CAR STOP 20 SOUTH JEFFERSON DAVIS PARKWAY
39 STATUE OF JEFFERSON DAVIS

This statue of Jefferson Davis, by sculptor Edward Valentine, was dedicated in February 1911. Davis (1808-89) was the president of the Confederate States. He died here in New Orleans in the Garden District (see the Payne-Strachan House on map 3), at the home of Judge Fenner.

CAR STOP 19 SOUTH LOPEZ STREET
40 SACRED HEART CATHOLIC CHURCH
3200 Canal

Sacred Heart of Jesus Roman Catholic Church was built in 1923 in the Italian Renaissance style. Flooding from Hurricane Katrina, followed by the archdiocese reorganization, closed this beautiful church.

Statue of Jefferson Davis, 1911

LEGEND TO MAP 13

CAR STOP 16
South Broad Street
41 VISTA TO FALSTAFF TOWER
CAR STOP 12
North Prieur Street
42 VA/LSU TEACHING HOSPITAL SITE

CAR STOP 16 SOUTH BROAD STREET
41 VISTA TO FALSTAFF TOWER

Look far off on the right, to the corner of South Broad and Tulane, and you will see the locally famous "Falstaff Tower" atop the old brewery, which closed in 1978. The orb on top and the lighted letters spelling FALSTAFF provided a weather forecast for residents since 1952. If the orb was green, fair weather was expected. Red forecast clouds, and flashing red and white signaled approaching storms. If the letters flashed from top to bottom, that indicated falling temperatures. Flashing from bottom to top forecast rising temperatures, and steady lights meant no change. Falstaff Tower was developed into apartments in 2010.

CAR STOP 12 NORTH PRIEUR STREET
42 VA/SU TEACHING HOSPITAL SITE

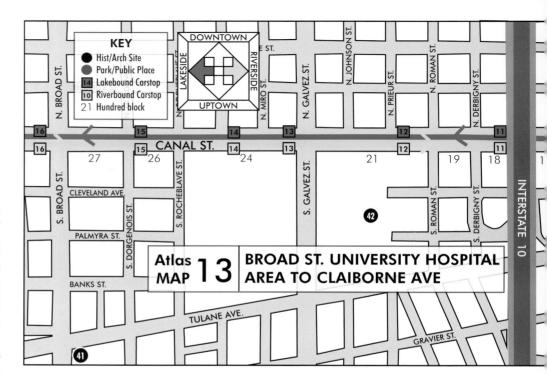

KEY
● Hist/Arch Site
● Park/Public Place
14 Lakebound Carstop
10 Riverbound Carstop
21 Hundred block

DOWNTOWN
LAKESIDE RIVERSIDE
UPTOWN

CANAL ST.

Atlas **13** BROAD ST. UNIVERSITY HOSPITAL
MAP AREA TO CLAIBORNE AVE

Joy Theater, 1947

CAR STOP 9 ELK PLACE
43 JOY THEATER
1200 Canal

One of several old theaters in this area, the Joy opened in February of 1947, closed in the 1980s, and reopened in 2011 as a music venue.

44 STATUE OF MOLLY MARINE

In the neutral ground of Elk Place is a statue dedicated in November 1943—a monument of a woman, "Molly Marine," in her service uniform. A local recruiter commissioned the statue to help recruit women during World War II.

CAR STOP 8 SOUTH RAMPART STREET
45 LOEW'S STATE THEATRE
1108 Canal

Built in 1926 as a part of the Loew's network, it remained a movie theater until the late 1980s. It became a concert venue until February 2007 and has been closed since.

46 ORPHEUM THEATRE
129 University Place

It was built in 1918 and opened for vaudeville acts as the RKO Orpheum in 1921. Not long afterward, it was changed to a movie house. In 1979 it became the home of the New Orleans Philharmonic Orchestra. Flooding during Katrina has kept its doors closed since.

CAR STOP 7 BARONNE STREET
47 WALGREEN'S DRUGSTORE
900 Canal

Its spectacular neon sign is a must-see at night.

48 ROOSEVELT HOTEL
123 Baronne

Originally the Gruenwald built in 1893, it became the Roosevelt in 1923 in honor of Pres. Teddy Roosevelt. The Fairmont chain acquired the hotel in 1965, but the Roosevelt name was restored in 2009 by the Waldorf Astoria chain. The lobby runs the entire block and is definitely worth the walk, especially when it is decorated at Christmas.

49 JESUIT CHURCH
130 Baronne

Across from the Roosevelt is the beautiful Immaculate Conception Catholic Church, known locally as Jesuit Church because it is run by the Jesuit priests. It opened in 1929.

50 GODCHAUX'S BUILDING
826 Canal

This department store was opened in 1844 by Leon Godchaux, the sugar-industry giant. Due to suburban growth and competition from the new, large retail malls, the store was closed in 1986.

CAR STOP 6 CARONDELET STREET
51 GUS MAYER BUILDING
800 Canal

Now a chain pharmacy, this building once housed Gus Mayer department store, which opened in 1900 and was part of 22 stores in the Southeast. If you look above the pharmacy's sign, you will see the original store's crest in a plaque marked *G/M*.

At this car stop, you may transfer to the St. Charles streetcar.

52 ADLER'S JEWELRY STORE
722 Canal

The clock outside is the most distinctive feature of this store, opened in the early 20th century.

53 PICKWICK CLUB
corner Canal and St. Charles

See 1 on map 1 for a description.

CAR STOP 4 CAMP STREET
54 SHERATON HOTEL
500 Canal

The streets change names as they cross Canal Street. Often the French-named streets are in the French Quarter and American ones, such as Camp Street, are on the uptown side. The uptown-lake corner of Magazine and Canal streets is where you could transfer to the #11 bus (MAGAZINE), which would take you directly to the Audubon Zoo.

CAR STOP 2 SOUTH PETERS STREET
55 HARRAH'S CASINO
8 Canal

CAR STOP 1 END OF THE LINE
56 WORLD TRADE CENTER
2 Canal

Opened in 1968, on New Orleans' 250th anniversary, this relatively new landmark stands virtually empty today.

This is the end of the Canal Street/Carrollton Avenue tour. At this car stop, you may transfer to the Riverfront Streetcar.

RIVERFRONT STREETCAR TOUR

The Riverfront Streetcar runs from Julia Street to Esplanade Avenue and the French Market area (car stops 1-8). For reference, this book considers eastbound cars going to the French Market outbound and returning inbound.

Established in 1988, it was the first new streetcar line in the city of New Orleans since 1926. Now using locally made streetcars, it began operation with 3 old Perley Thomas cars rescued from museums around the country. These 3 ran on an old railroad line with a track width that was different from the St. Charles track.

In 1997, NORTA wanted to connect the Riverfront line with the St. Charles line, in order to use Carrollton Station for overnight storage. So a connection had to be built at Canal Street. Also, federal law required that all cars on the line be handicap accessible. Rather than cutting huge holes in the sides of the antique cars, NORTA decided to build replicas using modern technology.

This chapter will not be a full-fledged tour, but more of an aid to get you where you want to go. A good walking tour of the French Quarter is available from Pelican Publishing Company. *Walking Tours of Old New Orleans,* by Stanley Clisby Arthur, is an invaluable guide for those who want to wander the narrow streets of New Orleans' Vieux Carré, or French Quarter.

LEGEND TO MAP 14

CAR STOP 1
Julia Street

1 RIVERWALK MARKETPLACE
uptown entrance

2 LOUISIANA CHILDREN'S MUSEUM
420 Julia Street

3 ERNEST N. MORIAL CONVENTION CENTER
900 Convention Center Boulevard

CAR STOP 2
Poydras Street

4 RIVERWALK MARKETPLACE
downtown entrance

CAR STOP 3
Canal Street

5 AQUARIUM OF THE AMERICAS
1 Canal Street.

6 SPANISH PLAZA

7 CANAL STREET FERRYBOATS

CAR STOP 4
Conti Street

8 WOLDENBERG PARK

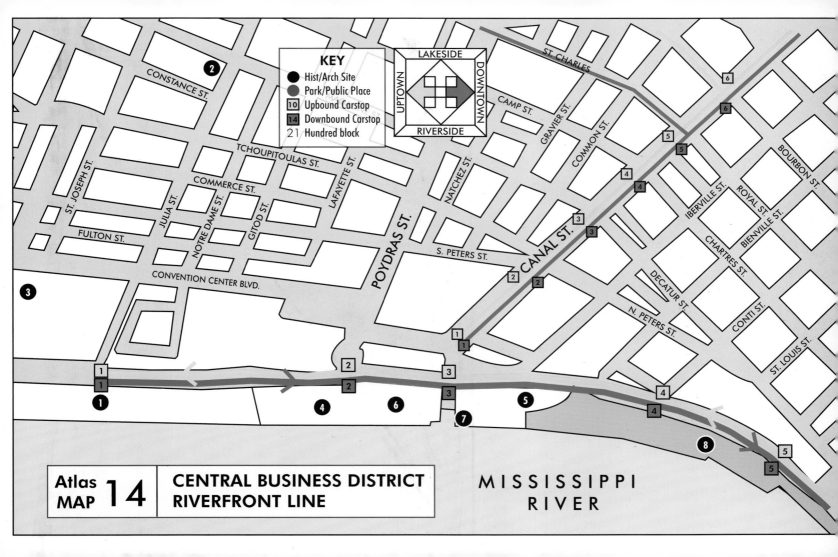

KEY

- ● Hist/Arch Site
- ● Park/Public Place
- 10 Upbound Carstop
- 14 Downbound Carstop
- 21 Hundred block

LAKESIDE
UPTOWN   DOWNTOWN
RIVERSIDE

CONSTANCE ST.

TCHOUPITOULAS ST.

COMMERCE ST.

ST. JOSEPH ST.

JULIA ST.

NOTRE DAME ST.

GITOD ST.

LAFAYETTE ST.

FULTON ST.

CONVENTION CENTER BLVD.

POYDRAS ST.

NATCHEZ ST.

S. PETERS ST.

CANAL ST.

ST. CHARLES

CAMP ST.

GRAVIER ST.

COMMON ST.

BOURBON ST.

IBERVILLE ST.

ROYAL ST.

BIENVILLE ST.

CHARTRES ST.

CONTI ST.

DECATUR ST.

N. PETERS ST.

ST. LOUIS ST.

Atlas MAP 14 **CENTRAL BUSINESS DISTRICT RIVERFRONT LINE**

MISSISSIPPI
RIVER

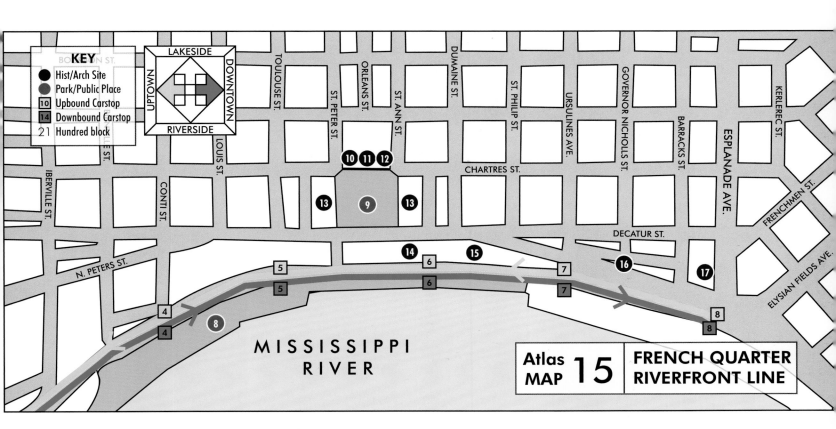

KEY

- ● Hist/Arch Site
- ● Park/Public Place
- 10 Upbound Carstop
- 14 Downbound Carstop
- 21 Hundred block

LAKESIDE

DOWNTOWN

UPTOWN

RIVERSIDE

BOURBON ST.

IBERVILLE ST.

BIENVILLE ST.

CONTI ST.

LOUIS ST.

TOULOUSE ST.

ST. PETER ST.

ORLEANS ST.

ST. ANN ST.

DUMAINE ST.

ST. PHILIP ST.

URSULINES AVE.

GOVERNOR NICHOLS ST.

BARRACKS ST.

ESPLANADE AVE.

KERLEREC ST.

FRENCHMEN ST.

ELYSIAN FIELDS AVE.

CHARTRES ST.

DECATUR ST.

N. PETERS ST.

MISSISSIPPI RIVER

Atlas MAP 15 FRENCH QUARTER RIVERFRONT LINE

LOYOLA STREETCAR TOUR

Like the Riverfront chapter, this chapter will be an aid to get you where you want to go. The Loyola line runs approximately 1 mile uptown, serving the New Orleans Public Library, Hyatt Hotel, Mercedes-Benz Superdome, New Orleans Arena, and New Orleans Union Passenger Terminal (Amtrak and Greyhound station). It begins at Canal Street and Elk Place.

Loyola Avenue has to hold the record for most name changes, as the same street has 9 different names. Beginning at Lake Pontchartrain as Marconi Drive, it becomes Orleans Avenue, Basin Street, Elk Place, Loyola Avenue, Simon Bolivar Avenue, LaSalle Street, LaSalle Place, and finally Burthe Street, ending at the Mississippi River.

Union Passenger Terminal

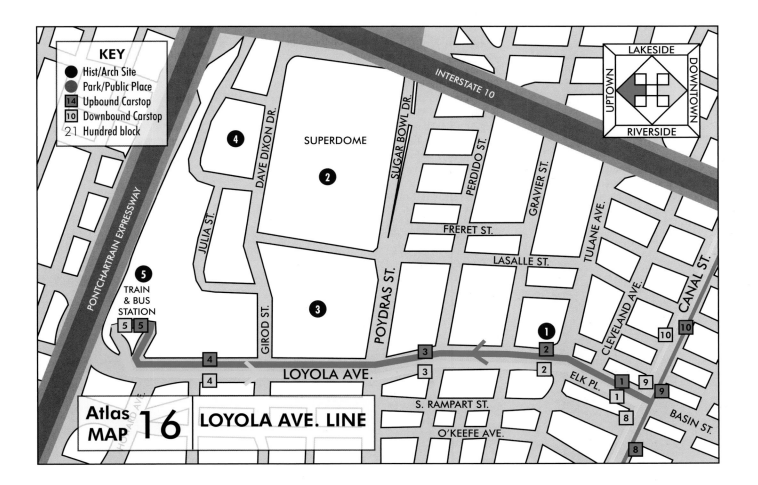

KEY

- ● Hist/Arch Site
- ● Park/Public Place
- 14 Upbound Carstop
- 10 Downbound Carstop
- 21 Hundred block

LAKESIDE
UPTOWN
DOWNTOWN
RIVERSIDE

INTERSTATE 10

SUPERDOME

DAVE DIXON DR.

SUGAR BOWL DR.

PONTCHARTRAIN EXPRESSWAY

JULIA ST.

GIROD ST.

POYDRAS ST.

PERDIDO ST.

GRAVIER ST.

FRERET ST.

LASALLE ST.

TULANE AVE.

CLEVELAND AVE.

CANAL ST.

TRAIN & BUS STATION

LOYOLA AVE.

S. RAMPART ST.

ELK PL.

BASIN ST.

O'KEEFE AVE.

HOWARD AVE.

Atlas MAP 16

LOYOLA AVE. LINE

CAR STOP 2 TULANE AVENUE
1 NEW ORLEANS PUBLIC LIBRARY
219 Loyola

The main branch of the New Orleans Public Library was built in 1958. It has 3 main floors and 2 subbasements and provides the system's largest collection of popular and research sources.

CAR STOP 3 POYDRAS STREET
2 MERCEDES-BENZ SUPERDOME
1500 Sugar Bowl

Formerly known as the Louisiana Superdome, this magnificent structure, built in 1975, is home to the Super Bowl Champion New Orleans Saints, the Allstate Sugar Bowl, BCS Championship games, and Tulane football.

3 HYATT HOTEL
601 Loyola

Opened in 1976 as a part of the Superdome complex, it suffered severe damage in Hurricane Katrina. The grand reopening occurred October 2011. Directly in front of the Hyatt Hotel, in the neutral ground at Loyola Avenue and Poydras Street, is the Cancer Survivors Plaza (park). Completed in August of 1995, it was designed by Milosav Cekic of Austin, Texas. It features a walkway formed by 14 25-foot columns that represent different world cultures, emphasizing the universal fight against cancer.

CAR STOP 4 JULIA STREET
4 NEW ORLEANS ARENA
1501 Girod

CAR STOP 5 HOWARD AVENUE
5 UNION PASSENGER TERMINAL
1001 Loyola

New Orleans' train station, known as Union Passenger Terminal, opened in 1954. It now serves 3 Amtrak train lines and the Greyhound bus line. It is worth a walkthrough to see the history of Louisiana and New Orleans in murals. Done by artist Conrad Albrizio, these murals were restored after Hurricane Katrina.

BIBLIOGRAPHY

Costa, Mary W. "The Freedmen's Bureau." Unpubl. MS., Tulane University, 1977.

Chase, John Churchill. *Frenchmen, Desire, Goodchildren, and Other Streets of New Orleans.* Gretna, LA: Pelican, 2012.

Christovich, Mary Louise, Pat Holden, Betsy Swanson, and Roulhac Toledano. *New Orleans Architecture Vol. 2: The American Sector.* Gretna, LA: Pelican, 1998.

Federal Writers' Project of the Works Progress Administration for the City of New Orleans. *New Orleans City Guide.* Boston: Houghton Mifflin, 1938.

Guilbeau, James. *The St. Charles Streetcar: Or, the New Orleans & Carrollton Rail Road.* Gretna, LA: Pelican, 1975.

Hardy, D. Clive. *The World's Industrial and Cotton Centennial Exposition.* New Orleans: The Historic New Orleans Collection.

Hennick, Louis C., and E. Harper Charlton *The Streetcars of New Orleans.* Gretna, LA: Pelican, 2012.

"Historic Districts Landmarks Reports," *Preservation,* November 1979, p. 2.

Kirk, Susan Lauxman, and Helen Michel Smith. *The Architecture of St. Charles Avenue.* Gretna, LA: Pelican, 1977.

Kolb, Carolyn. *New Orleans.* New York: Dolphin, 1974.

Landon, Ray. *In the Heart of Carrollton.* By the author.

Lemann, Bernard, and Samuel Wilson, Jr. *New Orleans Architecture Vol. 1: The Lower Garden District.* Gretna, LA: Friends of the Cabildo & Pelican, 1971.

Masson, Ann M., and Lydia H Schmalz. *Cast Iron and the Crescent City.* Gretna, LA: Pelican, 2011.

New Orleans Chapter of the American Institute of Architects. *A Guide to New Orleans Architecture.* New Orleans: New Orleans Chapter of the American Institute of Architects, 1974.

Samuel, Martha Ann Brett, and Ray Samuel. *The Great Days of the Garden District.* 5th ed. New Orleans: Parent's League of the Louise S. McGehee School, 1978.

Tassin, Myron. *The Last Line: A Streetcar Named Saint Charles.* Gretna, LA: Pelican, 1973.

The Sewerage and Water Board of New Orleans. *The Sewerage and Water Board of New Orleans.* New Orleans: The Sewerage and Water Board of New Orleans, 1978.

Wilson, Samuel, Jr. A *Guide to the Early Architecture of New Orleans.* Louisiana Architects Association, et al.

INDEX OF ADVERTISERS